The church in the West is experiencing seismic  gives us a prophetic glimpse into how they will Jack Magruder have done a brilliant job of iden that need to take place in the Western church nities and the world. Each of these fifteen chap. book. Every church leader should read *Missional Moves*, because it is a rare book that combines theological integrity and great practical application for accomplishing the mission of Jesus.

—Dave Ferguson, lead pastor, Community Christian Church;
spiritual entrepreneur, NewThing

This is an outstanding book. There are some who seem quick to abandon established churches, jettisoning their dormant potential. What Rob and Jack have done is not just to tell a captivating story but to present a compelling future for churches that lack missional imagination. What if we were able to reignite the people in our pews to join God, each day, in his mission in the world he so loves? What if our churches, long asleep, were awakened to a new, bright reality? *Missional Moves* is about this journey. I could not recommend it more highly.

—Mike Breen, founder/global team leader, 3DM

Missional Moves is one third courageous church *rethink*, one third brilliant leadership systems *reload*, and one third faithful biblical *resolution* to be the church we were all meant to be a part of. I applaud this book and pray that its story will influence your story.

—Hugh Halter, author, *The Tangible Kingdom*;
AND: The Gathered and Scattered Church; and *Sacrilege*

Rob and Jack have been early students and practitioners in the missional movement. They've done their homework. They are experts in this field. And they are also living it. This book belongs on every pastor's shelf!

—Shawn Lovejoy, lead pastor, Mountain Lake Church;
directional leader, *churchplanters.com*; author, *The Measure of
Our Success: An Impassioned Plea to Pastors*

Genuine "missional moves" of any magnitude are enormously complex and require immense leadership. When those two converge on a foundation of cultural, philosophical, and theological reflection that end up getting written down? You end up with the volume in your hands. The contribution that this book makes is original, seminal, and incredibly important.

—Dr. Ron Martoia, transformational architect;
founder, *velocityculture.com*; author, *Transformational Trek Tribe*

Missional Moves takes on practically all the major philosophical and practical challenges and changes associated with mission at this time in the church's history. It's a unique book—part pastoral inspiration, part apostolic insurrection, part how to build an atomic bomb. Amazing!

—Don Golden, Vice President of Church Engagement, World Relief;
coauthor, *Jesus Wants to Save Christians*

If you're wrestling with the tension between missional and attractional, and ready to move beyond conceptual conversations to faith in action, read *Missional Moves*. These guys are among the trailblazing churches that are modeling what church as movement looks like.

—Tony Morgan, author, leadership coach,
consultant (*TonyMorganLive.com*)

Every now and then a book comes along that challenges commonly held paradigms and paves the way toward a new normal way of thinking. *Missional Moves* is such a book. Wegner and Magruder have very carefully and graciously challenged what we have always thought about church missions, and they have redefined success and effectiveness for a whole new generation of churches. *Missional Moves* isn't based just on hopeful thinking or unproven theory; both authors have their feet on the ground seeing these shifts in play throughout the world.

—Tim Stevens, executive pastor, Granger Community Church;
author, *Vision: Lost and Found*

A tour de force, *Missional Moves* is an invitation into new frontiers of mission in a radically changing world. I highly recommend it.

—Stephan J. Bauman, president/CEO, World Relief

A picture is worth a thousand words. The words in this book will create pictures of missional moves you won't see anywhere else. Rob and Jack don't offer us a fantasy world of CGI make-believe; they offer a realistic look at what could be, and should be, in the world of missional moves. This book is a must-read for those who must see how God's kingdom is coming.

—Mark Beeson, founding pastor, Granger Community Church

MISSIONAL MOVES

Other Books in the Exponential Series

foreword by **ALAN HIRSCH**

MISSIONAL MOVES //

15 tectonic shifts that transform churches, communities, and the world

ROB WEGNER + JACK MAGRUDER

ZONDERVAN®

ZONDERVAN.com/
AUTHORTRACKER
follow your favorite authors

We want to hear from you. Please send your comments about this book to us in care of zreview@zondervan.com. Thank you.

ZONDERVAN

Missional Moves
Copyright © 2012 by Rob Wegner and Jack Magruder

This title is also available as a Zondervan ebook. Visit www.zondervan.com/ebooks.

Requests for information should be addressed to:
Zondervan, *Grand Rapids, Michigan* 49530

Library of Congress Cataloging-in-Publication Data

Wegner, Rob, 1970—
    Missional moves : 15 tectonic shifts that transform churches, communities, and the world / Rob Wegner and Jack Magruder.
        p. cm.
    ISBN 978-0-310-49505-5 (softcover)
    1. Missions—Theory. I. Magruder, Jack, 1974— II. Title.
BV2061.W44 2012
266—dc23   2012018606

Cover design: *Studio Gearbox*
Interior illustration: *Dustin Maust/Maustcreative*
Interior design: *David Conn*

Printed in the United States of America

13 14 15 16 17 18 19 /DCI/ 20 19 18 17 16 15 14 13 12 11 10 9 8 7 6 5 4 3

To Michelle,
the love of my life and my lily among the thorns
—Rob Wegner

To Sami,
my best thought and brightest star
—Jack Magruder

CONTENTS

FOREWORD

I have no doubt that the nest of foundational theology, paradigm shifts, and key ideas that together inform, shape, and constitute what we call the missional movement represents the only viable future for biblical Christianity in the Western world. I, along with many of the key church leaders and thinkers in our time, believe this is undeniable. Taken as a whole, Christianity is on the retreat in every Western cultural context. Witness the wholesale decline of biblical Christianity in Europe, Australia, Canada. In Europe alone, the birthplace of Christendom, Christianity is all but extinct.

This secularizing phenomenon can also be seen in the population centers of America, previously considered a bastion of Christianity in the West. Churches on the East Coast, in the Pacific Northwest, and even in the Midwest are all experiencing trended decline. Whether we like it or not, the principles, methods, and thinking about the church that worked in the past and were well-suited for the past are simply unable to address the complex context of the twenty-first century. They no longer square with our situation and the profound challenges it represents to us. This decentering means that the forms of the church produced when the church was at the cultural center of society—what historians call the Christendom paradigm—are fading, and we are now entering what sociologists call a post-Christian culture.

This is a radical shift that necessitates an equally drastic modification in the way in which we go about being a people faithful to Jesus and his cause. It can no longer be business as usual. The naive expectation that a simple reappropriation of well-worn formulas will produce a revitalization of the church, faith, and mission is not only foolish but can actually jeopardize the mission of God.

This does not mean that the gospel has lost its power. Far from it. The gospel of the kingdom remains the sole source for the wholesale renewal of the entire cosmos, let alone of society and the human heart. But these massive cultural shifts do mean that the commissioned carrier of the gospel—the church—must now find new and more fruitful ways to meaningfully deliver it to a needy world. This is what the missional church seeks to achieve—a recalibration of the church around the eternal purposes of God in and through the church of Jesus Christ.

This is no small task. It requires that we reconsider just about everything we've been doing, especially our culturally relative ways of doing church. Old habits of thinking and patterns of behavior must be thoroughly audited and evaluated to see if they are still consistent with God's purposes in and through his people. This requires theological imagination (to break the hold of the old paradigms and usher in the new), missional leadership (to negotiate change and be able to lead God's people into their own future), and courage (in the face of opposition both within and outside of the church). It will also require a serious commitment to ecclesial experimentation and innovation.

Granger Community Church in South Bend, Indiana, is a

church that has risen to this challenge. Rob Wegner, Jack Magruder, Mark Beeson, Tim Stevens, and the other senior leaders at Granger embody the kind of imagination, courage, and leadership needed in the church today. With holy joy I have observed and at times even participated in what they are doing. In this book you will encounter leadership that has a clear vision of the future, a willingness to take risks and put the system on the line to achieve that vision, a great change process that enables a megachurch (and they are that!) to move to a missional mindset, and a capacity to create working models of church that ordinary people can live into.

Rob and Jack have been at the heart of this ecclesial re-architecting. They are joyous, humble, intelligent, compassionate, and highly committed disciples of Jesus. They are the right men for the job. It is my hope that with this book, Rob and Jack's influence will extend to the broader church and provide many with a model of apostolic leadership, sorely needed in our day, and a model of the missional church that can advance the cause of Christ in our time.

—Alan Hirsch, founder of
Forge Missional Training Network

INTRODUCTION
A Reverse Tsunami

We've traveled to India more times than we can remember. Both of us lost count when the red ink from the Indian Customs stamps in our passports bled into the myriad others. But one of the most memorable trips—one that stands out abruptly—took place shortly after the tsunami hit the southeastern coast of India in 2004. On December 26 the world watched in horror as a massive tsunami destroyed more than 250,000 lives and rocked more than eleven nations. There, on the ground, we saw firsthand the absolute devastation wrought by this seismic event. We were taken to places and told, "Here is where the village used to be. Everyone was washed out to sea along with all of their homes."

The whole world stood in awe at the destruction wrought by waves of water that overturned cars, destroyed homes, and killed thousands of people. But following that first tsunami of destruction and devastation came another tsunami—not of death and destruction, but of unprecedented generosity and compassion. As the waters receded, millions of people flooded the land with acts of kindness and sacrificial service: feeding the hungry, clothing the naked, and building homes for the homeless.

What we have here are two types of tsunamis.

The first wreaks devastation and destruction. Caused by earthquakes resulting from the collision of tectonic plates, it is the product of an explosion of energy equivalent to 23,000 Hiroshima-type atomic bombs.[1] Yet as powerful as this tsunami of destruction can be, we want to suggest that the opposite—a tsunami of love and service—can be even more powerful. We call this a reverse tsunami.

Imagine a tsunami that, rather than leaving orphans when it recedes, leaves every child loved and with a family. Imagine a tsunami that, when the waters flow back out, sweeps away hunger. Imagine a tsunami that sweeps away every form of injustice: slavery, sex trafficking, racism, and generational poverty. Imagine a tsunami that sweeps away every disease. Imagine a tsunami that sweeps away all spiritual darkness and oppression, where every person knows the joy of redemption and salvation, where the song "Amazing Grace" is on the lips of every tribe, every tongue, and every nation.

In the prophecy of Habakkuk, we find a vision like this:

> For the earth will be filled
>> with the knowledge of the glory of the LORD,
>> as the waters cover the sea.

> —Habakkuk 2:14

Habakkuk is captured by a vision, not of destruction and death, but of God's global glory. This is a flood that brings healing to the nations. It is a tsunami of transformation, where the eternal realities of heaven and earth meet. But how does this transformation begin? Like all tsunamis, it begins with an earthquake. "After the Sabbath, at dawn on the first day of the week, Mary Magdalene and the other Mary went to look at the tomb. *There was a violent earthquake*, for an angel of the Lord came down from heaven and, going to the tomb, rolled back the stone and sat on it. His appearance was like lightning, and his clothes were white as snow. The guards were so afraid of him that they shook and became like dead men. The angel said to the women, 'Do not be afraid, for I know that you are look-ing for Jesus, who was crucified. He is not here; he has risen, just as he said'" (Matt. 28:1–6, emphasis added).

The earthquake that morning was unlike any before it, nor has there been anything like it since that day. It was an event that shook not only the city of Jerusalem but the entire cosmos—and the reverberations continue to resound throughout history. The tectonic plates of life and death collided into one another on Good Friday, but on that Sunday morning, the power of death itself slid under the rule and reign of Jesus Christ. Life overcame death in a release of resurrection power, and a tsunami of grace was released from the empty tomb, enough to cover and break the power of sin and bring transformation to all who believe the good news.

The resurrection is more than an escape hatch for us, where we hide while the rest of creation goes to hell. No, the resurrection was a *generative* event, the beginning of a new world—the kingdom of God—a world that is growing all around us, every day, even as the old world dies and fades away. The inauguration of the age to come and the renewal of heaven and earth was decisively launched when Jesus shook the earth and walked out of that tomb. The resurrection of Jesus also gave birth to a new people, the church. As the people of God, we are invited to join Jesus by living into this new world as he renews his creation through the transformation of human lives. We are invited to join his revolution, a fight that will defeat the powers of death and destruction and bring this new world into the here and now.

For this reverse tsunami to be unleashed, however, the effects of that Easter morning earthquake must shake and shift the tec-tonic plates in the hearts of Jesus' followers. When these plates shift to align with God's purposes, an unprecedented explosion is unleashed. These tectonic shifts, changes that we can make to conform our lives, our churches, and our communities to the mission of God, are what we call *missional moves*. In this book, we will discuss fifteen missional moves that fall into three different categories.

The first category of moves leads to a *paradigm shift*. Mark Twain once said, "You can't depend on your eyes when your imagination is out of focus."[2] The first moves we must make feed our vision and our imagination so that we can see beyond the status quo, beyond what the church currently is to what she can be. Like the disciples walking with Jesus on the road to Emmaus, we are blinded by preconceived notions that keep us from seeing where God is already present and working in our world. In this first section, we'll break bread and pray that God will open our eyes to see the resurrected Savior and his church in new ways.

The second category of moves involves what we call a *centralized practice shift*. If you're reading this book, it's likely that you are leading an organized local church that you care passionately about. You gather each weekend "inside the box" for corporate worship and teaching. Over the last fifty years, the church-growth movement has tried to transform what we do inside the box. A growing number of churches long for the same type of innovation to be expressed *outside* the box. Local churches are no longer content just sending checks and short-term mission teams as an expression of their commitment to God's mission. In this section, we'll dive into the missional moves that will unleash a local church on God's mission, both locally and globally.

The third category of moves follows the second and leads to a *decentralized practice shift*. Ultimately, Jesus designed his church to be a grassroots movement. As important and essential as organized expressions of the local church are, they cannot fully express all that God is doing in the world. Local churches typically focus on mobilizing their people around the church's centralized mission. But in addition to this centralized mission, we must learn to see where God has already mobilized his people to engage in mission in every domain of society. Every follower of Christ has a unique calling that may call them to follow God beyond the budget, goals, or infrastructure of the local church. In this section, we'll explore the missional moves that are a catalyst for unleashing an unstoppable movement of the people of God on mission, both in your back yard and around the world.

Please know this is a book written by practitioners for practitioners. It's a book birthed by a local church for the purpose of resourcing other local churches and new church plants. Everything written here has been worked out through the blood, sweat, and tears of the people of Granger Community Church, whom we (Rob and Jack) have the privilege of calling our family. As members of the leadership team at Granger (Rob since 1992, Jack since 2002), we continue to stand in awe of the audacious faith, daring courage, and faithful obedience of its people and leaders.

In addition, we are among a growing tribe of churches who are heading off the map into new territory through an experience called EnterMission Coaching. This is a learning community of kingdom revolutionaries who have committed to walking with one another in step-by-step contextualized application of the fifteen missional moves we have outlined in this book. EnterMission seeks to cultivate grassroots movements that implement small, focused, bottom-up solutions to the world's biggest problems — all through the local church. As you read some of their stories, we hope you'll follow your reading of this book by joining an EnterMission Coaching Hub. This book is a manifesto for that movement, a letter for the global underground church, and you are invited to join.

By God's grace, we pray this book will be a catalyst for a divine earthquake in your heart and at the core of your church, one that releases a reverse tsunami of God's resurrection power. We'll see you in the water!

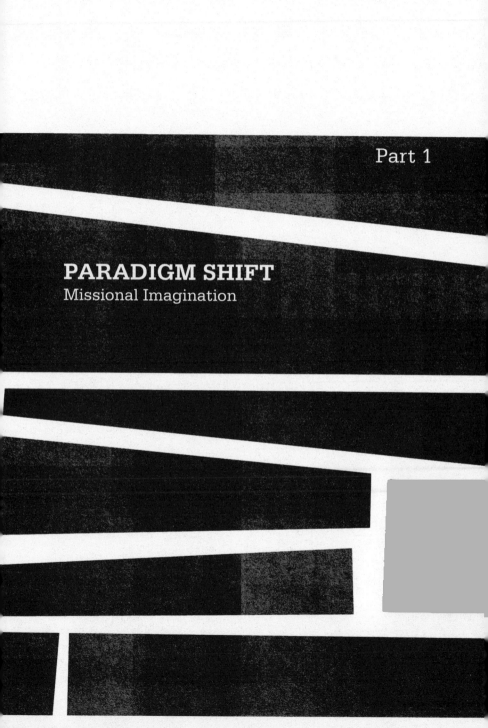

Part 1

PARADIGM SHIFT
Missional Imagination

In the Western church, we tend to be very pragmatic. If you're like us, you'll want to jump straight to the last two sections, where we break down the nuts and bolts of how to "get 'er done" as a local church on mission. But the truth is that we will never arrive at meaningful pragmatics without first experiencing a paradigm shift. Your church is currently operating on an underlying paradigm. Do you even know what it is?

You might assume we're talking about your statement of belief or a similar document that was likely hammered out in the early days of your church. But that's not what we're talking about. Bill Easum, in his book *Unfreezing Moves*, describes a paradigm this way: "Our paradigm is our repeated life story that determines how an organization feels, thinks, and thus acts. This systems story determines the way an organization behaves no matter how the organizational chart is drawn. The paradigm explains and then it guides behavior, and because of this it is the primary template that shapes all other things. Restructure the organization but leave the original paradigm in place and nothing changes within the organization."

So what's the life story of your church? It's a combination of the beliefs and values you hold; the metaphors you use; and how you tell your origin story, your hero stories, your victories and tragedies. It's what gives shape to your daily practices and your future dreams. That's your paradigm.

"What is the most revolutionary way to change society? Violent revolution? Gradual change? Neither. If you want to change society, then you must tell an alternative story," said Austrian philosopher Ivan Illich. That's the purpose of this first section: to discover your story as a church. And one of the best ways to understand and critique your own story or paradigm is by hearing the stories of others. How do you change your church? Change your story. Each missional move in this section introduces you to a different story. There are five stories in all: a gospel story, a story of mission, a bridge-building story, a family story, and a story of poverty leading to wealth.

Pay attention to how these stories interact with or even confront your story. Along the way, ask Jesus, "How do you want to change my story?" Or better yet, "How do you want to change our story?" Prayerfully consider the possibility that parts of your story may be too small, that it's time to stretch and expand the story you are currently living in.

Paradigm Shift

1. From Saved Souls to Saved Wholes
2. From Missions to Mission
3. From My Tribe to Every Tribe
4. From OR to AND
5. From the Center to the Margins

Chapter 1

FROM SAVED SOULS TO SAVED WHOLES
Missional Move 1

What is the gospel? This is the most important question a local church must answer. To put it lightly, the word *gospel* is a big word. In fact, you could argue that it's in the running for the title of Biggest Word in the Entire Lexicon of the Human Language.

Just how big is it?

While on vacation a number of years back, I (Rob) took my kids to the circus for the first time. One of the clowns dragged a huge trunk out into the middle of the center ring. He opened it up and began pulling out enough clothes to fill up a bin at the Salvation Army store. Then he pulled out four chairs, a table, and a huge feast of food to place on the table. Just as we thought he was finished, he reached in and pulled out an entire army of clowns, who filled up the center ring. My kids, who were little tikes at the time, were spellbound. My daughter asked with wonder, "How does he do it, Dad?" It was a magical moment. That is, until I responded, "There's a hole in the floor."

My wife slugged me.

What if I told you that the gospel is so big you could pull the transformation and healing of the entire cosmos out of it? What if the gospel is so big you could pull the redemption of every tribe and every nation out of it—billions of transformed people?

Unlike a clown trunk, there's no catch to the gospel, no gimmicks or hole in the floor to fool you into believing something that isn't real. The gospel is worthy, like nothing else, of genuine, childlike, spellbound wonder. That's why our first missional move begins with the expansion of our understanding, communication, and embodiment of the gospel.

The very first missional move that any church can make is to expand the gospel from a message of saved souls to one of "saved wholes." We've experienced the power of this simple but powerful tectonic shift here at Granger. Over the past decade, Granger has seen thousands of people released on mission, involved in redemptive movements both locally and globally. These include expressions like the Monroe Circle Community Center (something we call MC3), a hub for neighborhood renewal in the inner city of South Bend. It includes a movement of more than one thousand reproducing church plants in southern India, churches that are now becoming hubs for community development. Granger also has had the privilege of coordinating church-planting movements in places like Sudan, China, and Cambodia, where an additional one thousand new church plants have joined partners, pastors, planters, and people on the ground in each of those locales to work together for the advancement of God's kingdom. And it all starts with this first missional move. If we miss this one, none of the others will be effective. But if we get this one right, it will become the impetus and sustaining force for all of the other moves we make.

The truth is that for far too long we've settled for a wafer-thin, low-calorie, radically reduced understanding of the gospel. We call this the Saved Souls Gospel.

SAVED SOULS GOSPEL = THE PLAN OF SALVATION

For many churches, the gospel is only about saving souls. Whether it's presented as four laws in a tract handed to someone or preached as a fire escape from hell through a walk down the aisle, it presents a quick solution that solves the problem of securing your final destination for eternity. It's a gospel that sounds something like this: "God loves you and has a wonderful plan for your life. But you have a problem with sin and death. Jesus died on the cross to take care of that problem. Accept Jesus and you'll have forgiveness of sin and assurance of a place in heaven when you die." Sometimes this summary is called the Plan of Salvation, and to be clear, we do not intend to diminish or downplay the truth contained in this summary. We thank God that in Jesus we can be washed clean from sin. We thank God that in Jesus we have the confident hope of life eternal beyond the grave. It's not that this version of the gospel is incorrect or untrue. It's just incomplete.

We notice this when we study how Jesus communicated the gospel. He described it using two simple words: *good news.* "The time has come.... The kingdom of God has come near. Repent and believe the good news!" (Mark 1:15). However, many of us assume Jesus really meant to say, "The time has come. Heaven is available to all who accept me in their heart as their personal Savior. Believe the four spiritual laws, say the sinner's prayer, and you will get a cosmic Get out of Jail Free card when you die."

Without minimizing the message of personal salvation and our need for forgiveness of sins and the promise of eternal life, we still want to stress that this is not the *whole* story. The problem with the Saved Souls Gospel is that it is primarily concerned with our future in heaven. But is that all there is to the good news that Jesus came to share? By contrast, the Saved Wholes Gospel is concerned about both heaven *and* earth, and is a story that ends with the ultimate merging of these two worlds. Jesus' good news—his "gospel" message—was an announcement of a new social, political, religious, artistic, economic, intellectual, and spiritual order. A revolution had begun that ultimately would give birth to a new world, the kingdom of God.

SAVED WHOLES GOSPEL = JESUS IS LORD!

A robust understanding of the gospel includes three elements: the whole story, the whole expression, and the whole life.

The Whole Story. Jesus is the center of the story of God. All of creation and the story of Israel find their fulfillment in Jesus. At his return, Jesus will bring about the consummation of God's plan to heal and redeem the entire creation. Jesus has created an alternative covenant community of people, the church, who are called to join God in this great work. Before Jesus, Israel was designed to be this new community. Since Jesus, through his saving work on the cross, all are invited to join, not based on their merits but by God's grace.

The Whole Expression. The gospel announcement "Jesus is Lord" includes both a verbal proclamation and a demonstration proclamation.

The Whole Life. The gospel announcement "Jesus is Lord" is what some have called a three-word worldview.[1] The lordship of Jesus requires that the life and mission of Jesus be expressed in every area of life.

More extensive scholarly analysis of this idea can be found in the works of N. T. Wright, Scot McKnight, Dallas Willard, Timothy Keller, Alan Hirsch, Brian McLaren, and a host of other contemporary church leaders. Our goal in presenting this first missional move is to present some ways of making a more comprehensive understanding of the gospel portable at the grassroots church level. To do this, we begin by explaining how the statement that "Jesus is Lord" affects the story that we live and the expression of that story in all of life.

THE WHOLE STORY

The gospel makes sense to us as "good news" only if we first understand that the gospel belongs to a much bigger story, the biblical narrative. We can call this sweeping biblical narrative God's story, and we would argue that the gospel only makes sense when it is announced as part of God's story. This story has six parts: Creation, Rebellion, Redemptive Covenant Community, Christ, Church, and Re-creation.[2]

1. Creation (Genesis 1–2). God creates us and makes this world as his temple.[3] He places humanity there as his image bearers and representatives, to serve as co-creators, priests, and kings.

2. Rebellion (Genesis 3). Humanity rebels, bringing decay and death. Now disharmony and separation crack our relationship with God, creation, each other, and even our own selves.

3. Redemptive Covenant Community (Genesis 4–Malachi 4). God works out a way of transforming these broken people by covenanting with them. Israel is invited to join God in his plan to redeem all nations and all things, but they lose sight of this mission over and over again. Ultimately, they end up in exile. To reclaim a people to fulfill this mission, God sends the one great Israelite, the true Israelite, Jesus Christ.

4. Christ (Matthew–John). When Jesus speaks of "good news," he is tapping into the entire story of redemptive history up to that point in time. Simultaneously, he is also reaching out to God's future, the re-creation of all things, when the world will finally be as it should be.

In the time of Christ, the hope for the Messiah reaches a fever pitch. Why? For four hundred years the Jews have been waiting with an intense longing and frustration and expectation for the story of God to be fulfilled in the Messiah.

At the synagogue, after the inauguration of his ministry at his baptism, Jesus reads these words from the prophet Isaiah: "The Spirit of the Lord is on me, because he has anointed me to proclaim good news," and then says, "Today this scripture is fulfilled in your hearing" (Luke 4:18, 21). The "good news" tied into all of the Jews' deepest hopes and imaginations and sense of identity. Jesus is saying to them, "The story is all coming true in me. Right here. Right now."

Jesus begins to preach the "good news of the kingdom" and to demonstrate it with his life and his miracles. Through his death and resurrection, Jesus blows open the doors to the kingdom for anyone to come in. That leads us to the last two parts of the story.

5. *Church (Acts – Revelation).* Israel was designed to be the community that God would use to bless the world. In his life, Jesus fulfills God's intentions for Israel. Through the saving work of Jesus on the cross, all people are now invited to belong to the people of God. Their acceptance is based not on their ethnicity or their merits but solely on the saving work of Jesus' life, death, and resurrection. Jesus has created the church for the universal mission of making disciples in all nations and manifesting the kingdom in all of the earth. The Bible makes the audacious claim that the Spirit of Jesus is now physically present on earth through this new community, through his body, through the church. As the church, the body of Christ, we represent Jesus in our words and actions, and in this sense serve as the hands and feet of Christ.

6. *Re-creation (Revelation 20–21).* We now wait for the return of Christ. The full healing of the world will be completed only at the return of Jesus. At the second coming, evil will be judged and decisively defeated. In the words of Jesus, "I am making everything new!" (Rev. 21:5). Heaven and earth will collide and commingle. The world will finally be as it should be.

This is God's story. History is really his story. And Jesus is the central character, the hero of God's story. We believe that the gospel can be fully understood only within the telling of God's story, but to be clear, we are not suggesting that God's story and the gospel are the same. Some have suggested that this six-part retelling of God's story (or some other version of it) is actually the gospel. But the gospel is an announcement, a declaration that Jesus is Lord. This gospel announcement includes both a verbal proclamation and a demonstration proclamation, and as we announce that Jesus is Lord, in both word and deed, we find the whole expression of the gospel.

THE WHOLE EXPRESSION

Local churches are filled with well-meaning Christians who would disagree with what we are saying about the gospel. Because many in the church have been taught only the Saved Souls version of the gospel, they are convinced that the gospel is about only one thing: How do we get out of trouble with God? John Ortberg refers to this reductionist understanding of the gospel as "the minimal requirements to get to heaven when we die."[4] But when we study the Scriptures, we find little evidence that Jesus ever talked about this.

If this wasn't what Jesus preached, what did he talk about? What is the gospel Jesus preached?

> "After John was put in prison, Jesus went into Galilee, proclaiming the good news of God. 'The time has come,' he said. 'The kingdom of God has come near. Repent and believe the good news!'" (Mark 1:14–15).

> "Jesus went throughout Galilee, teaching in their synagogues, preaching the good news of the kingdom, and healing every disease and sickness among the people" (Matt. 4:23).

> "Jesus went through all the towns and villages, teaching in their synagogues, preaching the good news of the kingdom and healing every disease and sickness" (Matt. 9:35).

> "After this, Jesus traveled about from one town and village to another, proclaiming the good news of the kingdom of God. The Twelve were with him" (Luke 8:1).

> "When Jesus had called the Twelve together ... he sent them out to proclaim the kingdom of God" (Luke 9:1–2).

> "The Lord appointed seventy-two others and sent them two by two ahead of him to every town and place where he was about to

go. He told them ... 'When you enter a town ... tell them, 'The kingdom of God has come near to you'" (Luke 10:1, 2, 8–9).

When Jesus spoke and preached, he had one message that united all of his teaching. This was the message of "good news" that he shared wherever he went. In the Gospels, Jesus repeatedly links the phrase "good news" with the kingdom of God. In more than one hundred passages where Jesus refers to the kingdom of God, you quickly notice that the kingdom of God is the core of Jesus' message. It's more than a single volume on his proverbial bookshelf (somewhere between *Forgiveness* and *Money*). Rather, the kingdom of God is the bookshelf that holds all of the other volumes. The kingdom of God is Jesus' key paradigm. It is the framework that unites all of his teaching and preaching. All other topics are simply descriptions of or explanations about entering and living in the kingdom of God.

After rising from the dead, Jesus spent forty days with his followers. Ask yourself, If I had one month to live, what would I want to communicate to the people I love? It's likely that you would use this time wisely, passing along the things that you hold to be most valuable, the sacred and immutable message you want your loved ones to hear and understand. So what was this irreducible core for Jesus? "He appeared to them over a period of forty days and spoke about the kingdom of God" (Acts 1:3).

This is the very same message the early church carried to the world. The last glimpse we have of the early church in the last chapter of the book of Acts confirms this. The apostle Paul is under house arrest in Rome, and the book of Acts ends with this summation of the apostle's life and ministry: "For two whole years Paul stayed there in his own rented house and welcomed all who came to see him. He proclaimed the kingdom of God and taught about the Lord Jesus Christ—with all boldness and without hindrance!" (Acts 28:30–31).

For Paul and the early followers of Jesus, the message they shared—the good news of the gospel—came down to two things: the proclamation that "Jesus is Lord" and the proclamation of the kingdom of God. Because Jesus is Lord (the king and appointed ruler of the kingdom), these messages are essentially the same.

When you study what the Old Testament prophets say about the kingdom when it comes in its fullness, you quickly realize that in addition to the good news of the forgiveness of our sin and the promise of indestructible life beyond the grave (the resurrection), the good news is about far more than you or me as individuals. The gospel of the kingdom touches every sphere of human concern and engagement, motivating care for the poor, bringing justice to the oppressed, feeding the hungry, healing the sick, fostering education, providing decent housing, and creating art and beauty. The gospel changes everything.

Since the good news is about the kingdom of God, it helps if we understand what Jesus means when he talks about the kingdom. What is the kingdom of God, according to Jesus?

In Matthew 6:9, Jesus prays, "Let your kingdom come, let your will be done on earth as it is in heaven." The kingdom of God is the answer to Jesus' prayer. It's whenever and wherever God's will is done here on earth as it is in heaven. The kingdom of God is revealed whenever we join the work of Jesus in bringing what's "up there" down here. It's what the Old Testament prophets called *shalom*. *Shalom* is a Hebrew word that often is translated as "peace," but it refers to more than a vague sense of well-being. It speaks of the complete restoration of wholeness in every area of a person's life and surroundings. Neal Plantinga, in his book *Not the Way It's Supposed to Be*, describes the biblical idea of shalom: "The webbing together of God, humans, and all creation in justice, fulfillment, and delight is what the Hebrew prophets call *Shalom*. ... In the Bible, Shalom means universal flourishing, wholeness, and delight—a rich state of affairs in which natural needs are satisfied and natural gifts fruitfully employed, a state of affairs that inspires joyful wonder as its Creator and Savior opens doors and welcomes the creatures in whom he delights. Shalom, in other words, is the way things ought to be."[5]

We witnessed firsthand an illustration of shalom in an under-resourced community called Monroe Circle, a place where the people of Granger have been serving since 2002. It all began with two women and a man mentoring a handful of kids. Their personal involvement in the lives of these children snowballed into a movement that has led to the development of the Monroe Circle Community Center, a ministry led by the people of Granger and several other community partners that offers a full range of initiatives targeted at breaking the cycle of poverty.

At a community gathering of people seeking the good of the Monroe Circle neighborhood, Joe Kernan, the former mayor of South Bend and governor of Indiana, politely interrupted the agenda and asked permission to speak. Mr. Kernan also happens to be the president of our local minor league baseball team (Go Silverhawks!), whose stadium is across the street from Monroe Circle and a stone's throw away from our community center. Mr. Kernan shared his thoughts about the evident transformation in the Monroe Circle neighborhood: "This morning my staff gathered to evaluate this season. At one point, I asked them about security. We've had more than two hundred thousand people move through the stadium this year. Security is fundamental to our success. Most people do not feel safe coming to the west side of South Bend. Security has been a reoccurring issue every year for years. Vandalism, break-ins, muggings, and so on. To my surprise, I was told by my management team that there hadn't been one car broken into this year. Not one person had been accosted. Not one incident. Not a single issue." He then explained, "My entire team agreed the reason behind this incredible change in security has been the existence and impact of the Monroe Circle Community Center. Over the last four years, we have seen a change happening at a fundamental level in Monroe Circle. Every year it just gets better and better."

Indisputable impact. That's shalom. It's "up there" coming down here. The Saved Wholes Gospel expands the good news of the

EnterMission Story // A Snapshot of Shalom
Dan Chaverin, Executive Pastor
Westside Family Church, Kansas City, Kansas

Westside Family Church, through a peer-based partnership with indigenous leadership in Thailand, has created New Life Home, a place where young prostitutes from the red-light district can find a new beginning. Dan Chaverin, executive pastor of Westside Family Church, says, "Among the most humbling experiences of my life was sitting with a group of four young Thai women at our New Life Annex in June. All of them had been discarded as human refuse from the brothels in Chiang Mai, too abused and diseased to be of further use. All of them were HIV positive. One was found living in a phone booth, another in a hospital after a suicide attempt. All had been rescued from prostitution, given a safe place to live, food to eat, and shown the unconditional love of Jesus Christ for the first time in their lives.

"As we sat with them, they made their jewelry (learning an alternative skill to prostitution), talked, laughed, and received encouragement and hope from a recent graduate from New Life Annex. A year before, one of the ladies had been similarly rescued from the red-light district with her infant, and was now being encouraged and equipped. She was well dressed, confident, and beautiful. The contrast between her and the new girls was striking — her transformation was simply amazing. Jesus had given her the ultimate makeover. She now serves on staff as a model to the new girls of the transformational ministry of the New Life Annex. We are seeing firsthand Jesus' life and redemption at work!"

kingdom to every dimension of human existence in tangible and practical ways.

In our experience working with churches across the country and around the world, we find that many churches have structured their life for the proclamation of the gospel in a very reductive way. They see proclamation as something that happens only at their weekend services, primarily through preaching and music. They view the gospel only in terms of a verbal proclamation. While the gospel is a message that we proclaim with words, we want to stress that it's more than that. Where is the rest of the good news that Jesus proclaimed? Often, some of the most powerful gospel proclamation happens outside the four walls of a church, and it happens not only through the words we share but also as we seek to be the hands and feet of Jesus, bringing the "up there" down here into our communities and the world. We call this *demonstration proclamation*.

When you put these two together, verbal proclamation and demonstration proclamation, you have an undeniable witness for the lordship of Jesus Christ. The Saved Wholes Gospel finds its context in the whole story, calls forth a whole expression, and finally, invites us to surrender our whole life.

THE WHOLE LIFE

The gospel confession "Jesus is Lord" is the shaping lens that influences every nook and cranny of life. In Western traditions, we tend to see "religion" or "spirituality" as a separate category of life that doesn't impact the other areas of life, but there are no such distinctions in the three-word gospel worldview, "Jesus is Lord." When we view our lives through this lens, we confess that there is no part of the world or of our lives that doesn't come under his loving lordship.

Subconsciously, many of us tend to think of life in terms of boxes. I have a box for my work life, my family life, my recreation life, my social life, my private life, my financial life, and every other area. Everything is compartmentalized. When we hear the Saved Souls Gospel, we understand the good news by adding some new boxes to our lives. We add a box for our church lives, our devotional lives, and perhaps a box for our ministry lives. Supposedly, these new boxes will bring peace and success to all of our other boxes, even though the boxes don't really overlap very much. The difficulty of all this is compounded when we read passages like Matthew

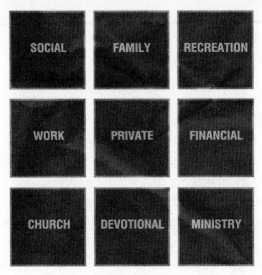

Figure 1.1

6:33, where we are commanded, "But seek first his kingdom and his righteousness, and all these things will be given to you as well."

If we've reduced the good news to nothing more than a message of individual salvation and a ticket to heaven, we read a passage like that and think, How am I supposed to do that, exactly? As followers of Jesus, we still feel overwhelmed by and dissatisfied with all of our boxes. Life feels like a juggling act in which we constantly try to keep all the boxes filled. But the box that contains my life doesn't get any bigger. I still have only twenty-four hours in a day. And now, I'm just squeezing more boxes in. This way of living is exhausting. Adding "Christian" boxes only seems to make life busier and more complex. Where is the easy yoke and light burden Jesus talked about?

Shortly after coming to Christ, my (Jack) wife's family attended a church where the standing order of the day was, "Follow God and God will take care of your family!" "Seek first" was equated with universal church attendance, volunteering for every expected activity, and a long list of rules to keep. Twenty years later, the fruit of following that message is not very encouraging. Many of the children who were raised in that environment, now grown adults, want nothing to do with the church. They were raised in an environment where "seek first" was compartmentalized from the rest of life, and they have since dismissed their parents' influence in their everyday lives.

Because our culture has a natural tendency toward dualism (dividing life into sacred versus secular spheres), when we add the Saved Souls version of the gospel into the mix, we end up with a Savior whose influence extends only to the "sacred" boxes of our lives. Churches everywhere are filled with people who are quite comfortable trusting Jesus with the spiritual areas of their lives and their future in heaven, but they fail to trust him in the day-to-day decisions they make. They have not integrated their faith and have failed to live out the good news that Jesus is Lord—over every area of life.

In Hebrew tradition, there is a well-known prayer called the *shema*. The *shema* comes from Deuteronomy 6:4: "Hear, O Israel: The LORD our God, the LORD is one." This was the basic confession of Israel's faith. The *shema* was the centerpiece of the morning and evening prayer. It encapsulated the oneness and the presence of God, directly confronting the box mentality that we tend to embrace. The people of Israel, like all people, were used to serving a different god in every box of their lives. But this new declaration meant that there could no longer be a different god for each box of their lives. The *shema* was a call away from idolatry, a confession that Yahweh was the Lord who ruled and reigned over every area of life. Israel's good news was that Yahweh, the one who had saved them from slavery in Egypt, would be the center of every area of life.

Our modern society is not all that different in this regard. Every culture, including our own, has its treasured set of idols. The box mentality is not unique to our time; it is our hearts' natural inclination to worship idols. Boxes are a convenient way of controlling our lives, and we all too easily set up a different god in every box. Often these idols compete with one another for our affection and allegiance. The only way out of this mess is bowing our knee and confessing that Jesus is Lord. Idols cannot simply be removed; they must be replaced.

"Seek first" is really an invitation—to dethrone our idols, smash the boxes, and make Jesus the center on which everything hinges. The strength of a wheel depends upon the strength of its center, the axle upon which everything turns. So what will be the center of your life? The good news isn't that Jesus offers you another box to add to your life. It's that he came to destroy the boxes and give us a new operating system, a whole new framework for seeing life. "Seek first" is not only an invitation to make Jesus first; it's an invitation to make him the center.

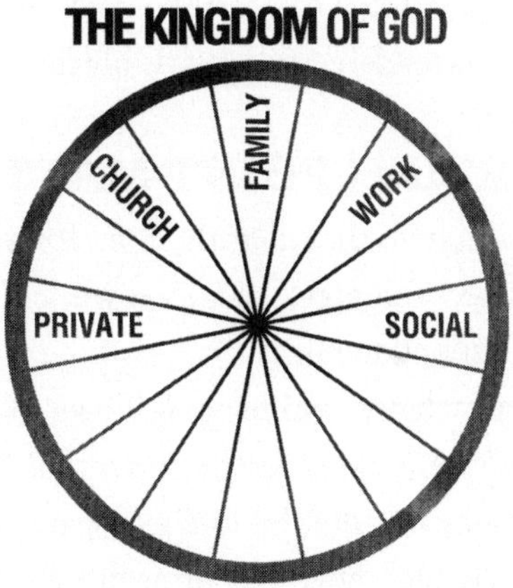

THE KINGDOM OF GOD

Figure 1.2

If we picture the kingdom of God as a wheel, then the three-word worldview that Jesus is Lord is right at the center. The spokes that radiate out from the wheel are the different areas of our lives. As the wheel rolls, the road may be smooth or rough, but our gospel worldview holds every area of life together and the kingdom rule of Jesus is manifested in every area of life. Like spokes radiating outward from that center, everything relates, rather than competes.

The sun is the center of our planetary system. Every planet orbits around the sun and is held in its gravitational sway. For centuries, humanity assumed that the earth was the center of the cosmos.

When Copernicus demonstrated that the sun is really at the center, he put the earth in its proper place.

Today, a raging battle takes place in each human heart. It's a battle over the answer to a question: What will be at the center? At the end of this age, there will be a Copernican-like revelation in which humanity will finally see that the center of all things has always been the one who made all things, the one in whom all things hold together. That center is Jesus, the Lord of all, the Alpha and Omega, the First and the Last. He, and he alone, is worthy to be the center. The first missional move is expanding your understanding of the gospel from Saved Souls to Saved Wholes. This is good news because it confronts each of us with the basic truth about our lives: we find life only when we live surrendered to Jesus. Only he is Lord!

YOUR STARTING POINT MATTERS

It's much easier simply to maintain the box. It's a known quantity. Go to church. Tithe. Volunteer once in a while. Live your normal life with a bit of Jesus added in.

But think about what would happen if every Christ follower in the world suddenly responded to the truth that Jesus is Lord and received the kingdom rule of God into every area of their lives.

Every other missional move is contingent upon getting this one right. We need to understand the gospel in light of the whole story, embrace its whole expression in word and deed, and respond with our whole lives. Only the gospel has the power to transform our churches and our world.

Where you start—what you preach and teach—really does matter. The starting point matters because it sets the trajectory for all that follows.

When we start with Saved Souls, we naturally invite people to make a one-time decision. But when we start with Saved Wholes, we naturally end up inviting people to become Jesus' disciples.

When we start with Saved Souls, we invite people to a momentary transaction. When we start with Saved Wholes, we invite people to lifelong transformation.

When we start with Saved Souls, we confirm an individualistic understanding of faith. It's about me and my private faith. When we start with Saved Wholes, we call people into the community Jesus is building and invite them to join him in his mission to redeem all things. It's about us serving Jesus together.

So ask yourself, How are *we* articulating the gospel? How does our church communicate the good news?

We'll never see lives changed with transactional, one-time decisions that confirm people in their individualistic faith. But God has given us something better: a disciple-making, community-creating, life-transforming, world-transforming message that Jesus is Lord and he is at work in our world, changing everything.

Chapter 2

FROM MISSIONS TO MISSION
Missional Move 2

Few words have more baggage in the church than the word *missions*. What do you think of when you read that word? I (Rob) get thrown into a time warp. I find myself back in the early eighties, sitting in a pew during Sunday evening service. Up front stands a missionary wearing a plaid leisure suit circa 1972—no doubt a hand-me-down gift from a generous Christian presented to him upon furlough. He has the slide projector clicking and humming. We all know he's got the Sunday night slot because he didn't make the cut for Sunday morning. Each slide projected on the screen falls into place with a loud click-clack and is accompanied by scintillating commentary: "This is the foliage in Bolivia. You'll notice the natives. Usually they are naked, but we clothed them for this picture. Aren't you glad?" He snickers to himself and waits for the congregation to respond. There is nothing but awkward silence. I'm sure I can hear crickets chirping somewhere.

Sadly, this actually happened.

Watching this slideshow left me with the clear understanding that missions was for two distinct categories of people: (1) hyperactive Christians who don't have anything better to do and (2) full-time professionals who are socially awkward and probably couldn't quite make it serving a church here in America. In other words, the last thing I ever wanted to be was a missionary; it was right up there in my list of dream jobs with landmine deactivation specialist. Rather than becoming a missionary, I hoped to groom a mullet, learn to play guitar, and become a rock star.

But everything changed a few years later. I had an experience that suddenly made the idea of being a missionary seem like a worthwhile pursuit. Like millions of other people over the last forty years, I went on a short-term missions trip.

The defining moment happened a few weeks into the trip. For the very first time, I'd come face-to-face with malnourished children. These weren't pixilated images on a TV screen but flesh-and-blood children right in front of me. On the trip, we had seen evidence of spiritual darkness, people still living in fear of ancient gods whom they had to appease. The exposure to the people and the culture was starting to work on me. That's when I snapped.

It was market day in Huehuetango, Guatemala. All the vendors had their stalls set up around the village square. The anchor of the square was a huge cathedral. At the foot of the church was a merchant who was selling strange masks and other bizarre items. I asked my pastor, who grew up in Guatemala, "What is that stuff?"

He said, "These are items the people use to worship idols, demons, and ancestors."

Surprised and shocked, I asked, "Why is it here? Right in front of the church?"

He replied, "When the priests came, they didn't ask the people to give up their false gods. They just added Jesus to the list. So in this cathedral, you will have one person praying to a dead ancestor, another person worshiping the god of fertility, another person praying to Mary, and another praying to Jesus."

I was dumbfounded. How could all of that be happening inside a church?

As I was thinking about all of this, my concern suddenly became very specific. While serving that summer, I had met a young boy named Willison who became my shadow, following me everywhere I went. Now, for the first time, I began to think about his life from an eternal perspective. I realized, like a bolt out of the blue, that if someone didn't do something, Willison might end up wasting his life on something less than Jesus. I was captured by the cosmic significance of God's love for this one little boy. And as we drove away from the square, I began to weep as I looked out my window at the hundreds of people standing there. Until that point in the trip, I hadn't really noticed the people. They could have dropped off the face of the earth and I wouldn't have cared a bit. But on that day, in an unexpected way, my heart began beating with the heartbeat of God.

I began to comprehend the canyon-sized gap between how I saw the world around me and how Jesus saw the world. And I have not been the same since. That day, I decided I wanted to care about the things that really mattered to God. The mission that Jesus gave his followers became my mission, and I wanted to love and serve the people he gave his life to redeem.

Despite the breakthrough I experienced that day, it took me several years to understand that what I experienced that day in the plaza was not "missions," it was the mission of Jesus. The distinction is more than mere semantics. It's the second missional move, another paradigm shift that alters our understanding of who God is, why the church exists, and how we should live in light of this. There is an imbedded cultural understanding of "missions" that keeps countless local churches sidelined from the actual mission of Jesus. Let's unpack the two primary understandings of "missions" and then look at what it means to shift from "missions" to the mission of Jesus.

"MISSIONS" = SPECIALIZED MINISTRY

Most of the time when the word *missions* is used within Christian circles, people are referring to the idea of mission as a specialization, the work of a select few, professionally trained individuals. Imbedded in this paradigm is the idea that the mission of Jesus really isn't for most local churches, and certainly is not for every follower of Jesus. This understanding feeds a hidden caste system, one that we not only accept but celebrate. Churches fund and send out ministry professionals with the specialized skills and training that enable them to carry out the mission of Jesus on behalf of the rest of us. Obviously, we need to be involved in some ways. We need to fund the work they do and help out when asked, in ways the missionaries define for us. But the bulk of the work falls to the ministry professionals. They carry out the real work of Jesus' mission.

Beginning with William Carey in 1792 and moving forward right up to the current day, dedicated men and women have stepped up to form centralized structures outside the local church, what we now refer to as sending agencies, parachurch organizations, and NGOs (nongovernment organizations). These organizations organize and send groups of Christ followers out to do the work of mission. And to be clear, we owe a debt of gratitude to these parachurch organizations for the phenomenal advance of the mission of Jesus throughout the world. One can't help but stand in awe at the number of missionaries sent, the languages in which the Scriptures have been translated, and the countless good works accomplished and lives transformed. Of the 2.3 billion people alive today who claim to follow Christ, the vast majority have come to the saving knowledge of faith in Jesus Christ thanks to the faithful work of these translocal expressions of the church. The debt owed to such ruthlessly sacrificial and dedicated people is incalculable!

On the downside, the transfer of the mission of Jesus from the local church to the parachurch has resulted in what Don Golden, vice president of World Relief, refers to as "the institutionalized

EnterMission Story // No More Farming Out Ministry
Brian Johnson, Pastor of Mission
Cornerstone Church, Auburn, Alabama

In light of missional moves we learned through EnterMission Coaching, we began a two-year process to trim down the edges and refocus not only our budget, but also our hearts and minds toward how we engaged our community in mission. Having a budget that includes forty local organizations really makes you feel like you are accomplishing a lot. We could clearly see that not only were we not accomplishing a great deal as a corporate body, but also because our resources were spread across such a large number of organizations, we were not empowering anyone else to accomplish a great deal either.

Over this journey we've been able to narrow our focus to six local agencies that we feel align with our mission, vision, and values. This focus allows us to advance the gospel together, and our congregation can/will plug in to a volunteer capacity on a regular basis. Through this process we have greatly freed up financial resources to reinvest in a new way.

To illustrate the change, the members of one of our small groups, who live in a low-income rural community, asked themselves, "What can we do here where God has already placed us?" The local school in their neighborhood had enacted a "Dress for Success" campaign without thinking through or fully recognizing how this would affect the children on the fringes in this rural community. Many of the female students were dropping out of school because they could not afford to meet the required dress code or were too embarrassed to admit that they could not meet the standard.

This group said, "Not on our watch. This will not continue." The micro-grant they requested from us was designed to help resource ten girls with clothing. But again, that's not all it does. They are now working with school administration and staff, counselors and local businesses to elevate the entire community involved. The group's ultimate goal is much broader than clothes. Their desire is to invest in these young women, to demonstrate unconditional love and be used in their lives however God leads them. Not a one-off event but a long-term investment in relationships.

We're not praying anymore about where we're going to send money next year. We're now praying for the believers who are in small groups together, that God would burden their hearts for places of darkness where they can shine the light of the kingdom and eradicate hopelessness. We are praying that the Holy Spirit would birth mission efforts that effect change never before seen in our community.

disempowerment of the local church." One of the hidden messages that has emerged from this defining structural paradigm for mission work is the idea that "mission is a specialization." In other words, "Don't try this at home, folks. Leave the real work of mission to the professionals." By and large, the church in the West tends to view the work of mission as something done by a special class of highly trained, privileged professionals: missionaries, agency professionals, and pastors. Alan and Deb Hirsch, in their book *Untamed*, describe the negative impact this paradigm of specialization has had upon the church:

> If one wanted to destroy the sheer transformative power of the body of Christ as a people movement, then the creation of the clergy-laity divide is nothing less than a stroke of demonic genius. One of the most catastrophic—heinous is not too strong a word—barriers to being a truly untamed church full of authentic disciples lies in the suppression of one of the most potent of Christian truths about the church—the priesthood of all believers. It is interesting that although Martin Luther rediscovered the potent aspect of New Testament teaching on the priesthood of all believers ... by and large, for Protestants and Catholics, it has remained a mere doctrine ever since. Every now and again it pops up—we would argue at every revival and renewal of the church—only to be suppressed again by the rise of religious professionalism (clericalism).[1]

Mission as specialization is one of the most powerful ideas suppressing the mission of Jesus in the church today. When we take that lid off, amazing things can happen. Once people taste the thrill of joining God on his mission, there's no turning back.

"MISSIONS" = MISSION AS SILO

"Missions as specialization" leads to a terrifying outcome: the paralysis of the vast majority of God's people. This problem leads us to our second paradigm for understanding missions. If the mission of God in the world becomes an area of specialization for a select few, then the scope of our participation in that mission will also narrow. In this sense, "missions" becomes defined by a silo mentality that reduces Jesus' mission to a department within the life of the local church. Rather than placing the mission of Jesus at the center of every local church, defining everything the church does, it becomes a "ministry area" within the church. Most churches today have a mission statement, and they talk about the importance of mission. But when you look at the day-to-day life of those churches, the mission of Jesus in the world is not the organizing principle of the church. Why is that?

A helpful way to grasp the problem is to think of a local church as a collection of silos (fig. 2.1). We have various departments in a church that operate somewhat independently from one another.

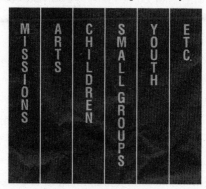

Figure 2.1

Sometimes these silos even compete against each other—for resources, people, platform announcement time, space in the bulletin, building usage, and of course, budget money. Each of them has a different mission or goal that they are trying to accomplish. One or more of these ministries will typically be categorized by the names *missions, outreach, evangelism, social justice,* or *compassion ministries.* Understood this way, "missions" is a line item in the budget, a committee, a collection of people on short-term trips or involved on volunteer teams, or a series of special offerings for missionaries working with pagans in foreign lands. Missions is just one more thing we do—right along with every other ministry of the church. If this describes you, we'd like to suggest that you drop the *s* and embrace the mission of Jesus.

WHAT IS MISSION?

You may have heard it said, "It's not that the church has a mission. It's that a mission has the church." This simply means that mission is designed by God to give the church its identity. Mission is *a priori* ("from what comes before") any expression of the church. God formed his people, first Israel and then the church, because of his mission. But when we operate with a "missions" mindset, we reverse the order. Instead of starting with God's mission, we begin with an *a posteriori* ("from what comes later") approach to the mission of God. To avoid this error, mission must "drop down" and become the foundation (fig. 2.2). The mission of God is the origin of every expression of ecclesiology, every understanding of how the church is structured and why it exists. Mission is the sweeping force that runs through everything we are and all that we do.

The people of God have always existed *because* of the mission of God and *for* the mission of God. Jesus did not come to earth to give us what we understand as missions; he came to give us one mission, the Great Commission. This understanding of mission breaks into three different dimensions:

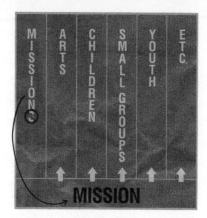

Figure 2.2

1. God on mission
2. Local church on mission
3. The people of God on mission

Let's look at how these three dimensions relate to one another and how together they form a biblical understanding of the one mission of God, given to the church—both corporately and individually.

GOD ON MISSION

If mission comes before church, then we should quickly add that God comes before mission. Mission starts with the understanding that the God we serve is a missionary. By his very nature, our God is a sending God. We see this expressed most clearly in the mission of the Son of God, who left his throne on a mission to redeem humankind and liberate creation from the curse. Mission is not something outside of God. It is part of his very nature, an expression of his heartbeat, his love.

Years ago, my oldest daughter and I (Rob) were snuggling on the couch one sleepy Sunday afternoon. She had crawled up and put her head on my chest. After lying quietly for some time, she popped up her head and asked, "Daddy, what's that noise?"

I said, "What noise?"

She pointed at my chest. "In there. That noise."

"That's my heart beating, baby," I replied.

A huge grin broke out across her face. She smiled as if she was the first person ever to discover the human heartbeat!

Over the next several moments, a question prompted by a book[2] I was reading at the time began to pound inside of me, "What would God's heartbeat sound like?" In my mind's eye, with my heart vision, I saw myself lying on the chest of God the Father, my Abba. I wasn't a grown man anymore. Just like my daughter, I was a child in my daddy's arms. With my ear placed right on his chest, I began to wonder, just as she had, "What will I hear?" And I sensed God speaking a four-word phrase, words similar to the words found in 2 Peter 3:9 and Matthew 18:14. They were repeated in rhythm, like a heartbeat: "That none should perish."

God promises that one day, every single people group on planet earth will dance to the rhythm of his heartbeat. In the future that God reveals to us, two rainbows will encircle the throne of Jesus — one made of light (Rev. 4:1–3) and the other made of people (Rev. 7:9–10). The first rainbow reveals the full spectrum of light, while the second reveals the full spectrum of ethnicity: people from every tribe, every tongue, and every nation. The earth will be lit by this rainbow of people living as the global family of God.

Stop for a moment to imagine this symphony of praise. Picture what it will be like when all of God's intended diversity is brought together in unity to bring maximum glory to the one who is worthy. There will be Native American people praising God with their tribal dances, together with Kalahari bushmen praising God in tonal languages. African Americans will sing their gospel songs with real soul next to white suburban guys (like us) trying simply to clap in rhythm.

One day, people from every one of the more than twenty-four thousand people groups in the world will be gathered into the kingdom (we will look more deeply at this in Missional Move 3). One day the Great Commission will become the Great Completion. That is God's mission in the world! And it is also the consummation of history—the goal of it all. God is building a family, a global family that will join him in the healing of the world. This mission heartbeat radiates from the Father, through the Son, into the Spirit-filled church, sending us out on mission to the world. The Father sent Israel. The Father sent the Son. And now the Father, Son, and Spirit are sending the church. This is the reason why our God left his throne. The heartbeat mission of God is what drives all of redemptive history.

Figure 2.3

The Father sent Israel. At a time when humans were alienated from God, through the covenant with Abraham and later with Israel, the Father himself came to man. Perhaps the most remarkable aspect of Yahweh's covenant with Israel was this gift of his presence, birthed of his sent-ness: "I am going to come to you" (Exod. 19:9).

God sent himself. Leading Exodus scholar J. I. Durham sees this gracious act of coming down as the most important event not only in Exodus but arguably in the entire Old Testament. He states: "The Sinai narrative has been determined by a single factor ... the gift of Yahweh of his presence to Israel."[3]

God invites Abraham and Israel to join his mission. They are given a missional blessing: blessed to be a blessing to all nations (Gen. 12:2–3). They are called as servants to bring about God's redemptive purposes in the world. For those of us who have a New Testament lens for the Scripture, the blessing in Genesis 12:2–3 is the Great Commission of Matthew 28:19–20 in raw form.

The Father sent the Son. The mission God gave to Israel, though never abandoned, was not fully realized until God sent his Son, Jesus. Through the life, death, and resurrection of Jesus—the perfect Israelite and the embodiment of God's purposes in Israel— God fulfills Israel's mission.

The Father, Son, and Spirit are sending the church. With Jesus' death and resurrection, the seed of the apostolic church placed in Israel at Sinai comes to fruition through the birth of the church. The church, filled with the Spirit, is now sent to represent Jesus by taking his message and his ministry to the entire world.

Today, the church is the primary means for God's mission in the world. The local church was created and designed to be a "sent" organism, not a stationary fortress unwilling (or unable) to go anywhere.

THE LOCAL CHURCH ON MISSION

So what has happened to the church? As we suggested earlier, a dichotomy exists between the church in its localized expression and the missionary expansion of Christianity as a larger movement. Within the church, we now have two separate structures, the congregation—what we call the local church—and what missiologists call the missionary society—the world of parachurch agencies, denominations, and other nonprofit structures that exist outside the local church.

One hundred years ago, the English missiologist Roland Allen first identified this growing divide between the local church and the missionary society. Allen wrote that the local church was designed to be the missionary society. The local church is God's plan A, his means of saving and redeeming the world, but since local churches lost sight of God's original intent, the missionary society, the parachurch world, stepped in to fill the gap. We believe that the parachurch and the local church can, in fact, work together in ways that amplify and enhance the impact of both parties. Later we'll spend an entire missional move unpacking how that has been realized in our context at Granger.

If your church is not advancing, it is not "on mission." And if it is not "on mission," it might not be a church. In the book of Acts, we see that the local church is the sender and center of mission. The early church had been "established and organized with a worldwide mission for a worldwide work."[4] The local church has always been intended to be the forward-advancing outpost for the kingdom of God at the absolute margins of our world, where God's light and life are not yet known.

A friend of mine (Jack), a pastor, recently told me that he didn't believe that his congregation would be on board with doing anything to alleviate the pain of the working poor in their community. In sad candor, he explained that his people were pretty sure that the church existed for the strengthening of Christians. I told him that he should probably consider taking the word *church* out of his organization's name. Puzzled, he asked me what I meant. I told him that what he was effectively being asked to pastor was a "club," not a church. A club can be about whatever you want it to be. It can be a bridge club, a baseball card club, a social club, or even a Christian club, but it's not a church. The church has a mission, given to it by God. And if your church has a different mission than the mission of God, you might want to rethink whether the organization you belong to is really a church.

We wrote this book because there is a growing groundswell of local churches that will not settle for anything other than doing mission. And like the team we serve on at Granger, countless local church leaders want to move beyond just doing mission—they want to reclaim a more primal biblical identity for their church as a *missional* church, a church on mission. That's good news! We are also finding organizations (some of whom we will talk about in this book) who understand this growing desire that churches have to reengage on the front lines of God's mission, and they are eager to help them do so.

The bad news is that such engagement is difficult, costly, risky, and often dangerous. Ask the martyrs who line the corridors of time. Like the little boy whose dreams of grandeur evaporate when he goes from playing "soldier" in his back yard to being dropped into an actual combat zone for the first time, the local church must learn to count the cost and realize that the shift from missions to mission will require stepping up in a profound way. The next section of the book, "Centralized Shift," will talk more about taking this necessary step to become a local church on mission.

THE PEOPLE OF GOD ON MISSION

The third dimension of mission involves more than applying the mission of God to local churches; it means incorporating God's mission into the whole life of every follower of Jesus. Every follower of Jesus is called to carry out the mission of Jesus in every area of life. At the church where we lead and pastor, we don't do "missions." Instead, we attempt to live out the mission of Jesus, creatively expressing who we are in Christ. In this sense, we can truly say that everyone has a life mission, and that life mission is found in the mission of Jesus.

What we call "life mission" refers to the personalized expression of God's mission in individual lives. Much of this will necessarily fall outside of the scope and focus of the centralized expression of the local church on mission. As we will see in Missional Move 7, for your local church's expression of mission to have power, it must be focused. However, we would urge caution here. The very focus needed to keep the local church on mission can sometimes exclude or disregard the life mission of God's people as individuals. It can unintentionally communicate to those involved in the local church: "If you're not doing our deal, you're not on mission." But nothing could be further from the truth. All of us are missionaries, and much of the mission work God is calling our people to do will not fit within the centralized ministry focus of a church. God has scattered his people into every domain of society. Your "life mission" starts at home, at work, and in the places where God has already mobilized you. God has plans for the local church and for each of us as individuals. The final section of the book, "Decentralized Shift," will be entirely devoted to the importance of unleashing the people of God on mission.

Before we conclude the second missional move, we want to show you how all three of these dimensions of mission combine into an unstoppable force.

APOSTOLIC MOVEMENT

When you combine the idea of a God on mission with the local church on mission and the people of God on mission, you have what Alan Hirsch refers to as an *apostolic movement* (fig. 2.4). What is apostolic movement? A "movemental" expression of the church in her most ancient, powerful, and radiant form, combining both multiplying churches (the local church on mission pictured as the round nodes) and multiplying disciples (the people of God on mission pictured as the X nodes) dispersed into every domain of society on mission. So, when both multiplying churches and multiplying disciples are happening simultaneously, transforming lives and culture

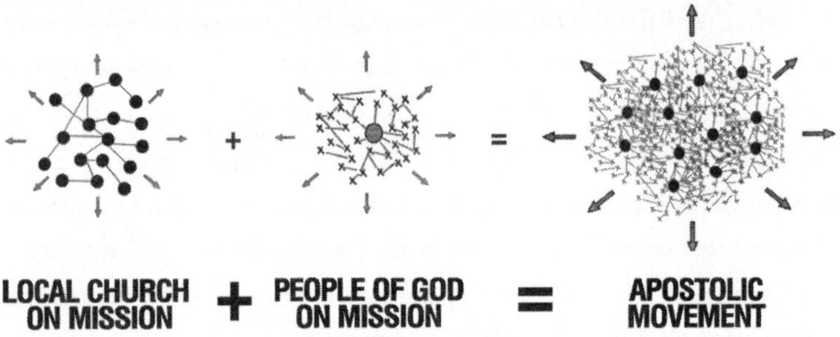

LOCAL CHURCH ON MISSION + PEOPLE OF GOD ON MISSION = APOSTOLIC MOVEMENT

Alan Hirsch and Dave Ferguson, *On the Verge* (Grand Rapids, Mich.: Zondervan, 2011), 74, adapted with permission.

Figure 2.4

through the gospel, the church recaptures her identity as apostolic movement. This is paradigmatically different than the predominant expression we see today, church as institution.

We'll look more deeply at apostolic movement, especially in the last section of the book, but let it be said for now that the church was never designed to be a fortress for the righteous; rather it was designed to be a flood of revolutionaries into every dark place. In the New Testament and in many places outside the Western world today, the church knows herself as an unstoppable grassroots movement, despite the great challenges of scarcity and persecution. The time has come for the church in the West to reclaim its scriptural identity as an apostolic movement. To do that, it must embrace its mission as the reason for its existence and stop thinking of "missions" as something reserved for the specialized few.

Most local churches choose a single-strand approach to mission. They choose either "bring them in" (grow the weekends and start multisites) or "send them out" (plant new churches and restructure around missional communities). In several of the next missional moves, we'll look at how to incorporate all of these strategies into a cohesive, synergistic approach, pointing the way toward the local church's becoming not just a reproducing church but a catalyst for an apostolic movement.

We live in a post-Christian, missionary context in the United States. And reaching people in this post-Christian culture will require more fluid forms and expressions of church. Only an apostolic movement has what it takes to turn the tide and reach our communities and our nation.

We must learn from our brothers and sisters in places like China and India what it means for the church to be an apostolic movement again. We need their leadership to shape our future! And they need us as well. There are no perfect expressions of the church, and many of these indigenous movements have viruses in them that keep them from robust health and vitality. Our journey has led us to the discovery that we need to learn from the non-Western church, and the church in the West has gifts of knowledge, training, and tools that can address the viruses that infect indigenous movements, providing a cure and building immunity against false teaching.

Today, we are at a historic juncture. If the church in the West jumps the curve to apostolic movement and effectively partners with other such movements around the world, we could see the glory of God cover every tribe, tongue, and nation within the lifetime of our children.

The vision of most local churches extends to the next calendar year; perhaps a truly visionary church will project its mission five or ten years out. Isn't it time for us, as leaders of God's church, to embrace a vision so huge that it would involve the next generation and even the next century? Let's reach toward a vision that will live a century beyond us.

Chapter 3

FROM MY TRIBE TO EVERY TRIBE

Missional Move 3

On a recent trip to Navy Pier, my wife, Michelle, and I (Rob) strolled through the Smith Museum of Stained Glass, the first museum in the US dedicated solely to stained-glass windows. The windows were all originally installed in Chicago somewhere, each window giving us a unique insight into the area's cultural and ethnic history.

As you might imagine, many of the windows are from churches, featuring scenes from the life of Christ. These mosaics of stained glass, hidden away from the bustling crowds, are truly breathtaking. I stopped for a moment to snap a picture of one of them in particular, and as I pressed in close, I could detect thousands of different fragments of glass, each embedded with its own unique color. Looking closely, you notice the individual fragments, but when you step back, you experience the full story that each window is telling—the full glory of the glass image. With each step backward, the thousands of tiny, diverse pieces became unified into a beautiful countenance, together forming the face of Jesus.

In that moment, I was struck by the realization that this mosaic of stained glass is itself a picture of God's plan and purpose for humanity. Each of those pieces of the mosaic represents a different culture, a different people group, and when we pull back, God's global glory is seen in the unity of all that cultural diversity.

This insight leads us to our third missional move, the shift from my tribe to every tribe. In God's kingdom, my tribe can only find its meaning within the context of every tribe. If a local church wants to be on mission with God, it must expand from the natural tendency to fixate on reaching its own tribe to the God-birthed and Spirit-fueled desire to see every tribe included in the kingdom.

Diversity and unity are essential to God's purpose for his glory. Scripture is clear that diversity and unity are the design of God. This relationship is seen in the diverse parts of the body of Christ unified in mutual membership and purpose. It is best seen in the kingdom diversity of every tribe, tongue, and nation unified around the throne of the King in the new heaven and new earth. God's intention was to create diversity so that our unity is not homogenous—a sea of similar faces—but rather a rainbow of cultures, languages, and appearances. We are a diverse people unified by one purpose: God's global glory, or what we call G3.

The flow of every expression of mission through the local church finds it place within the larger flow of G3. Without the larger map of God's global glory, individuals end up stuck in dead-end streets, and local churches find themselves circling in cul-de-sacs. In Jesus, reaching my tribe finds meaning only within the context of God's larger mission to every tribe.

THE STORY OF SCRIPTURE

In this third missional move, we want to take you on a journey through the storyline of the Bible. Far from a tiptoe through the tulips, this is an Everest expedition that will take us into the deep canyons and high summits of redemptive history. Our map: the Scriptures. Our compass: the Spirit. Our destination: God's global glory.

I grew up reading the Bible as sixty-six independent books with various messages, themes, and stories woven throughout them. This approach of segmenting the Bible tends to blind us to its larger message, and we often fail to recognize the map leading to God's global glory. Many of us grew up hearing the Bible taught to them as a series of short stories with moral lessons (perhaps supported by the amazing visual power of a flannel graph). To grasp the shift we are talking about in this missional move, we need to leave behind our modernistic approach to the Bible, where we atomize it into timeless principles, and take a broader, wide-eyed view. We must learn to make sense of the whole story, not just the mini-stories. The story of God's global glory is the Story of Stories, and it helps us frame the individual stories of the Bible within a larger map. We begin by looking at the Bible as one book with a single theme, one that starts in Genesis and runs through to Revelation.

THE SEED IN GENESIS

We find the seed of God's global glory buried deep in the soil of Genesis. What we know in the New Testament as the Great Commission appears both implicitly and explicitly in the book of Genesis. We find implicit references to it in Genesis 1:28 and Genesis 9:1, where first Adam and Eve and then Noah are commanded to "be fruitful and fill the earth." And this theme emerges even more powerfully in a climactic scene that unfolds at the Tower of Babel. The people of the earth have gathered together for the purpose of self-aggrandizement, seeking glory for themselves, and they are scattered by God for the purpose of his glory. John Piper summarizes God's purposes in this scattering when he says: "[God] was restraining evil by preserving diversity that would function as a check and balance in the human craving for power and fame and wealth. But in the same act of judgment he was preserving and increasing the diversity that would become the many-color mosaic of redemption. Evil would be deflected by diversity in language and culture; and the glory of Christ would be reflected by the diversity in language and culture."[1]

In other words, when God scattered the builders of Babel's tower, this wasn't just an act of punitive judgment; there was another purpose at work. It was, in fact, a strategic act of mercy that would later culminate in God's global glory. It was an act of mercy toward humanity because it restrained evil, blocking future attempts by human beings to create glory for themselves apart from God. The confusion of languages created a built-in system of checks and balances. Yet it was also a strategy designed to bring about the fulfillment of God's global glory. As we see later, at the time of Pentecost, the diversity of Babel is redeemed in the unity of the church, as the nations are brought together under one King, all for the glory of God (Acts 2:5–11). At Babel, the disruption of languages created confusion. At Pentecost, the translation of languages created fusion around Jesus and the gospel.

In the next chapter of Genesis, what has been implied throughout the text now becomes explicit, and the hidden seed of the Great Commission buried in the early stories of Genesis begins to break through the soil in Genesis 12. Here we find what some have referred to as the original Great Commission:[2] "The LORD had said to Abram, 'Go from your country, your people and your father's household to the land I will show you. I will make you into a great nation, and I will bless you; I will make your name great, and you will be a blessing'" (Gen. 12:1–2).

God said to Abram, "I'm going to make you a father of a great nation." But at the time God made this promise, Abram was about to hit one hundred and Sarah was never going to see ninety again. They might not have ultrasound machines, but they both knew the truth: Sarah wasn't having no babies. Abraham didn't have any Viagra.

Yet they didn't forget one simple truth: God is able. Abram heard a voice that made his soul tremble, the voice of God. It was a voice unlike any he had heard before, a voice of love and deep thunder. He heard the voice of the God of heaven, whose name was not yet known, say to him, "I will bless you." Five times. Bless. Bless. Bless. Bless. Bless. When God repeats a word so many times in such a small space, we know that word carries heavy freight. "I will bless you." If I were Abram, I'd probably envision a twenty-thousand-square-foot tent with ten rooms and four baths or the 2012 Lexus Camel (eight cylinders). I'd see my 401(k) retirement account filled with flocks of sheep. What Abram did see was children—descendants as numerous as the stars of the sky and the sand on the seashore.

"I will bless you," the voice said. But the blessing of Abraham was only the first part of the promise. It was a blessing filled with momentum, what you might call a "missional" blessing.

The message continued, "Look higher. Look deeper. Look farther. Look wider. With love I mean to bless you all. *All the peoples on earth* will be blessed with your blessing." That word *peoples* is not a typo. God's not just talking about lots of people; he's talking about people groups. *Peoples* refers to groups of people bound together by culture, tradition, and language. God invites Abram to see all the peoples of the world, many of whom would have been his enemies, and he says to him, "I'm going to bless you, not so you can be fat and sassy in your blessing, but for this purpose: to become a channel of blessing to all those other peoples."

The blessing of God breaks us free from our own ethnocentricity. Our default pattern is to look to our own interests: "My culture, my people are the greatest. We are the most important." But here, God is pulling Abram out of his native, human ethnocentricity into God-centricity, where every culture is celebrated and valued. God's plan in his promise to Abram was to design a new nation, a whole new people group, who would rise up—not to build a tower for themselves, but to lift their eyes to God and celebrate his glory, not their own. Abram is invited to see a new world, a place where people from every tribe and tongue come together in the blessing of God.

This was more than the typical "Bless me, God." Abram was invited to be involved in something never before envisioned, the global glory of God realized in the unification of human diversity under the reign and rule of a true king, a future descendant of Abram himself. Once Abram had this G3 map burned into his mind, he knew there was no choice but to head toward Canaan. Once you have the G3 map in your mind, you'll find yourself willingly going to places you never thought you'd be able to go, doing things you never thought you would be able to do.

TOP-LINE BLESSING AND BOTTOM-LINE RESPONSIBILITY

We like the way Don Richardson, in his book *Eternity in Their Hearts*, describes the promise that God gives to Abraham. Don says it this way: "Every Top-Line Blessing comes with a Bottom-Line Responsibility."[3]

Top-line blessing: "I will bless you."

Bottom-line responsibility: "You will be a blessing ... all peoples on earth will be blessed through you."

Richardson argues that the Abrahamic covenant forms the foundation for the entire story of Scripture. The top line of the covenant is God's promise to bless Abraham. Following that initial promise comes a second promise, one that carries a bottom-line responsibility of sharing God's blessing with all the peoples of the earth. Bob Sjogren further explains this idea: "The Top-Line Blessing and Bottom-Line Responsibility run throughout the Scriptures like a set of railroad tracks."[4] One rail is the top line. The other rail is the bottom line. Together they make up one story that stretches off into the distance. We must always balance these two tracks in our understanding of the Bible. If you raise one rail above the other, the train comes off the tracks.[5]

Once you learn to "see" the two tracks and recognize the G3 map, we guarantee you'll never miss it again. Sadly, most followers of Jesus live without this map, wondering why they have a surprising lack of direction, meaning, and purpose in their lives, even though they know Jesus.

So how do we internalize the map?

Lera Boroditsky, assistant professor of psychology at Stanford University, has spent extensive time traveling with a remote people group, a tribe with expertise in orienteering. As the editor of *Frontiers in Cultural Psychology*, her research has led to the discovery that some languages have curiously pigeon-like, directional power. She says, "Follow me to Pormpuraaw, a small Aboriginal community on the western edge of Cape York, in northern Australia. I came here because of the way the locals, the Kuuk Thaayorre, talk about space. Instead of words like 'right,' 'left,' 'forward,' and 'back,' which, as commonly used in English, define space relative to an observer, the Kuuk Thaayorre, like many other Aboriginal groups, use cardinal-direction terms—north, south, east, and west—to define space."[6]

The normal greeting in Kuuk Thaayorre is not "How are you doing?" but "Where are you going?" So you can't get past hello in this language without knowing which way you are facing. A common answer would be something like, "North northwest in the middle distance." Now you may wonder if people really respond with that kind of precision in their everyday conversation with one another. Professor Boroditsky clarifies, "It's actually more precise than that. There are eighty-some different choices!"[7] In other words, the Kuuk Thaayorre speak an orienteering language. And this phenomenon is more common than you might think. Of the seven thousand languages in the world, one-third of them have this "orienteering" property.

What is striking about the discovery of these languages and the people who speak them is that they have an ability that we might refer to as dead reckoning. "It's an ability, after any kind of circuitous path, they can turn around and find their way home. It's an ability that we thought was beyond human capacity — we had observed it in ants and in birds.... Birds have magnets in their beaks. Ants are counting their steps. Some kind of extra 'thing' that they were doing. But these are not folks who have magnets or ant super powers. They are using the same cognitive system we are using. They are just using it differently."[8]

So how do they do it? Ms. Boroditsky says it is really quite simple: "They are paying attention to something we don't normally pay attention to." She confesses, "My time there was socially awkward. People thought I was quite dim because I wasn't oriented and I didn't know exactly what direction I was headed or which way was which all the time. You can ask a five-year-old there, can you point northeast? They will point without hesitation. If you ask a Stanford or Harvard professor the same thing, they have no idea!" After spending a week with the Kuuk Thaayorre, however, the professor finally had a breakthrough. She was walking along one day, trudging through the sand and wondering if she was wasting her time there.

"All of a sudden," she says, "I noticed that in my head there was this extra little window—like in a video game. There was like a little console. In the console there was a bird's-eye view of the entire landscape I was walking on. I was a little red dot that was traversing that landscape."

She was amazed at the gift of her new eyes. She could see the entire map and her place in it. She concludes, "All of a sudden … I just saw it. It was just there. Then, I kind of shyly shared this with someone that this strange thing happened. They looked at me strangely and said, 'Of course, how else would you do it?'"[9] After that day, she began to pay attention to something she normally didn't pay attention to, and she found that there was a "console" in her mind. She could now "see" the map and found that she had a directional ability she had never known about before.

We have found that the G3 map to the Bible works like this. It provides a God-given sense of dead reckoning that will always lead you, in whatever section of Scripture you find yourself in, to recognize God's global glory. The key, then, is learning to pay attention to something we don't normally pay attention

> Want to unfold the G3 map further? Look for the ebook *The G3Map* at *missionalmoves.com*.

to. We need to discover the "orienteering" language of the Scriptures. Once you begin to speak this language and pay attention, you'll find the G3 map will turn on, and you'll never see the world the same again.

ORIENTEERING LANGUAGE

This illustration suggests that we have a few important "orienteering" words to master if we want to grasp the importance of the G3 map to the Scriptures. The words are *mispachot*, *goyim*, and *ethne*.

The first word we need to learn is *mispachot*, the Hebrew word for "peoples." We find it referenced in the bottom-line responsibility of God's promise to Abraham that "all *peoples* on earth will be blessed through you." The term has been variously rendered as *tribes*, *nations*, and *peoples*, and many English Bibles translate it as *families*. Some have even suggested that the best reading would be *communities*, which is a fascinating and important idea we'll come back to in a later missional move. When you look carefully at the three hundred usages of this word in the Old Testament, it usually describes a subdivision of a larger tribe or larger people group, a group that is larger than a household, but smaller than an entire tribe.[10]

When we look at places in the Bible that repeat or reiterate God's promise in Genesis 12:3,[11] we discover three additional passages where the word *mispachot* is replaced with the word *goyim*. This Hebrew word, *goyim*, is roughly equivalent to the Greek word *ethne*, the same word that Jesus uses in giving his followers the Great Commission in Matthew 28. It is frequently translated as "nations," but it isn't referring to our modern geopolitical nations. So what do *goyim* and *ethne* refer to?

When we think of nations today, we first picture a map with little lines drawn around a piece of territory. But that is *not* what the Bible is talking about. Jesus' primary concern in the Great Commission isn't with geopolitical nations. Nation-states come and go. In fact, Rand McNally now offers a globe with removable magnetic nations so you can replace the out-of-date nations with the latest names and property lines. But the word *ethne* points us toward the ethnicities—the languages and extended families that constitute the peoples of the earth. The terms *goyim*, *ethne*, and *mispachot* are all referring to similar groups of people, the "nations" (people groups) within the nations (geopolitical territories). Today, researchers have identified over twenty-four thousand tribes (people groups) among the two hundred geopolitical nations of the world. G3 vision expands your understanding of mission by broadening the scope of what God promised to Abraham and what he calls his church to in the Great Commission.[12]

As followers of Jesus, we embrace the "nations"—not just our own tribe but every tribe of the world—as our family. In fact, in Christ, my tribe is blessed so that I will be a blessing to other tribes. The words, "You will be a blessing," are not just a promise; they imply a responsibility that God places upon those who are blessed. This is clarified in the command that Jesus gives to his followers. It's more than the Great Suggestion; it's the Great Commission!

When we read the Bible looking primarily for top-line blessing for me and my tribe, we can remain largely unaware of our bottom-line responsibility and miss the G3 map altogether. This is where our orienteering language comes in handy. From now on, we'd encourage you to look for these key words (*nations, tribe, peoples, families*) in the Bible, both in the Old and New Testaments. You'll soon discover that this theme—of God blessing his people to be a blessing to the world for the sake of his global glory—runs through hundreds of passages and scores of stories you likely learned in Sunday school. In our rush to find moral principles for living, we hurry past the bigger story.

Now you know the rest of the story. And if you're willing to stop and notice, you'll begin to see how these two tracks, the top line and bottom line, run throughout the entire Bible, forming a backbone theme from their introduction in Genesis to the conclusion in Revelation.

THE FULFILLMENT IN REVELATION

Where do we find the climax of this story? It is described for us in the book of Revelation. "After this I looked, and there before me was a great multitude that no one could count, from every nation, tribe, people and language, standing before the throne and before the Lamb. They were wearing white robes and were holding palm branches in their hands. And they cried out in a loud voice: 'Salvation belongs to our God, who sits on the throne, and to the Lamb'" (Rev. 7:9–10).

When you and I finally stand before God with others from every tribe, tongue, and nation, Jesus will receive the glory he deserves from all of redeemed humanity. By unifying our diversity, God gets greater glory. One tribe short and Jesus will not have the maximum glory he deserves.

When you begin to see God's G3 map, you will begin to see the faces of the different people of the world. I like to think of the G3 map like a family photo that God keeps in his pocket. I (Rob) have a special family photo taken at Disney World's Magic Kingdom. At the moment we were taking the picture, a rainbow appeared right above my family. It was like God's smile over us that day. And what makes it special to me is that all of my kids are in the picture. I know that if any of my kids were missing from that photo, it would not be complete. I want every single one of my kids with me under that rainbow in the Magic Kingdom.

Jesus is building a new world within this world, but it's no "magic" kingdom. It's the kingdom of God, a kingdom with no end. And he wants his kids, from every tribe and every tongue and every nation, there under the smile of that rainbow. The kingdom won't fully come until every tribe is included. That scene we read about in the book of Revelation is nothing less that Jesus' family photo.

G3 AND THE LOCAL CHURCH

So what does all of this mean for the local church where you serve? To begin with, of the twenty-four thousand people groups that have been identified in the world today, approximately sixteen thousand of them are reached, which means that the people have a viable Christian witness. That's good news! But it also means that there are around eight thousand people groups still unreached, people who have never heard the good news about Jesus in their own language. They have never heard of God's stunning offer of amazing grace. Not ever.

The people of Granger Community Church are grateful to be collaborating with an indigenous church-planting movement on the bleeding edge of the Great Commission in the nation of India, and we'd like to tell you about one of our friends in that movement. Sathyea Sealin, like many church planters, is bivocational. During the week, he is a laborer, working eight to ten hours every day hauling, lifting, shoveling, or whatever other backbreaking tasks local landowners will pay him to accomplish on their land for a daily fee. Friday night after work, Sathyea packs up a few belongings, takes his Bible and a bamboo mat, and heads up the mountains to work among a community of people living along the jungle-thicketed mountaintops. Until a generation ago, these people used to live as forest nomads, moving hunter-gatherer style through the jungles to piece together their daily living.

Before Sathyea Sealin came to their village, they had never heard of Jesus. Shortly after he began his ministry, the wife of the head village elder became among the first to follow Jesus as her Savior and Lord. This elder has seen such a change in his wife that when Sathyea comes to the village, the elder tells his villagers, "Go meet with the Jesus man!"

In addition, this elder offers Sathyea valuable protection. Extreme communist guerillas have infiltrated the jungles surrounding this region, recruiting impoverished tribal villagers, providing training and weapons, and instructing them to shoot or capture any nontribal people who travel in the mountains. Sathyea explains, "The village elder was so amazed by the change in his wife's life that he has given me his protection. He has told me, 'You will always be safe. Anyone who is your friend is my friend.'"

While most of us here in the West, when faced with that kind of real and present danger, would tuck tail and run, Sathyea just smiles and continues his story. "There are eight villages I have already contacted in this region," he notes. "My aim in life is to see a movement of churches thriving in every village!" Sathyea gets it. It is not only about his tribe but also about every tribe.

For the first time in history, the church stands within distance of realizing the Great Commission. Throughout the ages, the gospel has been passed from generation to generation, and now the end is finally coming into view. Only one generation in all the ages will have the privilege of finishing the Great Commission. Two thousand years of saints and martyrs will lift that generation up on their shoulders as heaven's dream is completed. Could that moment finally be upon us?

Unfortunately, much of the church in America and around the world remains acutely unaware that we're in the final play of the game. Every year, our family watches the Super Bowl. Over a hundred million people gather to watch the game. But imagine this scenario. The game is on the line. The score is tied, fourth down. Two minutes remain on the clock. The ball is thirty yards from the end zone. The coach calls a time-out. All around the arena, fans jump to their feet and the crowd noise swells with anticipation as the final play is called. The huddle breaks and it's time for the players to take their positions—but they don't.

As millions of viewers watch, these titans begin wandering around the field. The fullback sits down and starts untying his shoe. A couple of the linemen drift toward the outraged crowd, taking off their helmets and pads. The coach runs onto the field, screaming at his players, "What are you doing? The clock is still running! We still have to execute the final play!"

Ridiculous? Absolutely. It would never happen on the football field. But right now, as the most important game in the world is being played, the church is preparing for the final play of the game. The ball is within reach of the end zone, yet most of the players are clueless about where they are on the field, what position they play, and how much time is left on the clock. Many of them do not even realize that the game is on the line. The arena they play in? The nations of the world. The end zone? The finish of the Great Commission. The team? Every member of the church.

From the book of Revelation, we know that God's global mission will one day be accomplished. It is going to happen. This has been God's plan all along, and what he first promised to Abraham in Genesis 12 will one day be completely fulfilled. Is your local church on the field, engaged in the game? Or are you still sitting on the sideline? A missional church will consider their involvement with unreached people groups a nonnegotiable. We agree wholeheartedly with Ed Stetler's summary: "So emphatic is God about his glory being displayed throughout the earth, that I don't think a church should call itself missional unless it is seeking to serve locally, plant nationally, and engage an unreached people group globally." Almost two billion people have yet to hear the gospel. It's time for a movement of local churches to rise up and declare, "We'll go to the hard places. We'll commit our time, our people, our prayers, our passion, and our resources to the nations that have yet to hear the good news. We will be a local church for the unreached people groups of the world. We're going to move the kingdom ball toward the end zone no matter what it costs us!"

So what engagement does your church have with unreached people groups? Are you ready to make the shift from your tribe to every tribe? Have you caught the vision for God's global glory? Maybe it's time to get in the game.

Chapter 4

FROM OR TO AND
Missional Move 4

There are two words that are being used to describe churches today, but it's not always clear what people mean when they use them. The first word is *attractional*. An attractional church values bringing people "in" to the church—attracting them. The faith community that we serve, started by Mark and Sheila Beeson in their living room twenty-five years ago, has blossomed into Granger Community Church, one of the most well-recognized attractional megachurches in America. Over the years, our local church has shown up on the "top hundred lists" of the most innovative, fastest-growing, and most influential churches in the country. Like most churches on these lists, we have mixed feelings about being recognized this way. But we mention this to make a simple point: if any church can be labeled attractional, it's Granger. Our detractors have called us "crazy church," "circus church," and even the "Chuck E. Cheese church." We've worked hard to make our church a place where people want to come, where they feel welcome and want to bring their friends and neighbors. That's what it means to be an attractional church.

The other word that people are using to describe churches today is one you are likely familiar with, since it's part of the title of this book—the word *missional*. A missional church focuses on sending people "out" to engage the community and world. Missional churches aren't as concerned with attracting people to a facility or a service. They emphasize the importance of meeting people where they are, going out into the workplace, into schools, and into the community and bringing the message and the ministry of Jesus to people, right where they are.

For the most part, a church tends to lean to one side or the other. A church is typically more attractional or missional, and many believe that picking one approach automatically requires that you are not the other. But that's not our experience, and we'd like to share another side to this story. As we mentioned, Granger is well-known for being an attractional church. In fact, we're an attractional church that became so attractional that we had to become missional. That last sentence may sound like a contradiction, so we'll explain what we mean in the pages to follow. As our story unfolds, we hope you'll find, as we have, that it's no longer necessary to choose sides and live under the tyranny of the *or*, choosing between being a missional church or an attractional church. We're convinced, both theologically and from our experience, that the idea of a church being both missional and attractional is possible. We must move from alienation to integration.

OPEN A CAN ...

Want to see a humorous portrayal of the differences between attractional and missional thinking? Check out this clip from 2010's AND Conference at *missionalmoves.com*.

FROM TRADITIONAL TO MISSION OUTPOST

Just more than twenty-five years ago, a young couple, Mark and Sheila Beeson, emptied out their bank account, packed up their kids and the few belongings they had, left the safety of a secure position within an established ministry, and came to Granger, Indiana, to start a new church. Mark and Sheila had both grown up in the traditional church, and while they had a deep respect for this legacy, they also sensed a growing discontent in their hearts. They saw the gap between the church and society and how more and more people were feeling alienated from the church.[1] Increasingly, they found that the church was for people who grew up in church. You had to know the church dress code, you had to know church language, you had to like church topics, and you had to know how church worked to really belong.

Mark and Sheila were determined to find a way to remove the cultural barriers that kept many people from meaningfully connecting with the church. They began asking questions like, "What if we could engage mainstream culture without losing our kingdom distinctiveness? What if we could

TWENTY-FIVE YEARS

Head to *missionalmoves.com* and watch the video "Granger Community Church: 25 Years in Review."

remove the extrabiblical church culture and speak the language of mainstream culture?" They began to communicate the gospel and present the person of Jesus in a culturally relevant way that was attractive to the people from the culture. And, indeed, people were attracted. The little faith community that started as a mission outpost in Granger has now blossomed into a megachurch with five thousand people gathering each weekend and more than ten thousand who call Granger their church home.

FROM MISSION OUTPOST TO MEGACHURCH

During my (Rob) senior year at Taylor University, Mark Beeson shared with me his vision for this new church. He said, "I don't want you to think about what we're doing as just church. We're planting a mission outpost for the kingdom of God in this town. If you want to join this team, you've got to be a missionary." I'd never heard a pastor talk like that before. When Mark described the job of a pastor as a missionary, I was hooked. There is a scene in the movie *Jerry McGuire* where Rene Zellweger's character says to the character played by actor Tom Cruise, "You had me at hello." Well, it's safe to say that Mark had me at "mission outpost." He has now been my mentor and coach these past twenty years.

My wife, Michelle, and I joined the team and we have never looked back. To be honest, there just wasn't time. We were on a mission. God was on the move. In those early days, we met in homes, a school, a fire department, and more than seventeen different rented facilities. There was the vibe of a growing movement, and we knew we were pioneers blazing a new trail for the kingdom.

Mark was actively involved in the process of shaping our culture and forming our DNA, steering us clear of the pitfalls of insular church culture. In many ways, the values that were formative in our early years clearly illustrate some of the key characteristics of an attractional church:

- *Outward Focus.* Mark would describe church in ways we'd never heard before. "We're not a church for churched people. We're a church for unchurched people. We're the church for the community." Our church wasn't made up of the "sheep shift" from other congregations. We weren't just stealing market share of the churched people in our community. We had freshly redeemed people everywhere. Most of us had never been in a church like this before. We were committed to reaching the lost and serving our community.

- *Cultural Relevance.* Mark would say over and over again, "We are going to leverage the arts and technology to communicate the timeless message of Jesus in a timely manner. Good missionaries study the culture, the language, and find points of meaningful engagement. Bad missionaries diminish or dismiss the culture like the colonialist missionaries who made the natives build little white churches with steeples, wear an English tie, and sing fourteenth-century European hymns."
- *Gifts-Based Ministry.* We helped people discover their God-given gifts and find a way to unleash that through service. We taught about the priesthood of believers on a regular basis and chanted slogans like "every member a minister!" As much as people slam the attractional church for being consumeristic, we had amazing percentages of people serving and still do. Thousands of people were serving both inside and outside of the box, both on campus and in our community.

These attractional values—things like cultural relevance, outside focus, and gift-based ministry—will bloom and grow in a healthy church. And as they grow, they form the seeds that are necessary to break down the dichotomy between attractional and missional. That was our experience at Granger—the values of attractional ministry contained the seeds of God's mission to reach the world and help us engage missionally. We found that incarnational impulses, typically associated with more missional churches, are actually buried within each of the values listed above. The attractional values that shaped how we did programming "inside the box" later exploded into missional expression "outside the box."

FROM MEGACHURCH TO MISSIONAL

This fusion of missional and attractional first appeared on two fronts, one locally and the other internationally. In 2002, the children living in the Monroe Circle neighborhood near our church were being crushed under the wheel of generational poverty. A decade later, parents in that same neighborhood now expect that their kids will go to college. Locally, we watched as God transformed into a real community what had been a forgotten neighborhood characterized by elderly, disabled, and radically low-income families (averaging less than $7,300 per year in household income).

Recently, a local principal was visiting a kindergarten classroom at one of the schools in our community, and she noticed that within the chaos of unruly behavior that is typical in city schools, there was a pocket of well-behaved, focused children. The difference was so noticeable, she was determined to find out what made those kids so different. What did she discover? These were students who had been involved in Granger's mentoring program, Son City Kids. That principal was so impressed that she sought out the leader of that ministry to find out how the school, our church, and the community center we had opened in Monroe Circle could partner together.

Where did all of this start? It wasn't a decision by one of the pastors at our church. Instead, it was a vision born in the hearts of two women and one man who had experienced firsthand the brokenness of generational poverty in Chicago, and felt God calling them to dedicate themselves to engage the children of Monroe Circle. They began to invite their friends to join them, and this snowballed into a micromovement of people in our church that now has a fully functioning community center as its hub. In this local context, working with the people in Monroe Circle, we learned what it means to engage in *incarnational mission*.

Internationally, we have had the privilege of being invited into direct relationship with a grassroots, indigenously led church-planting movement in India. In this setting, under the mentorship of indigenous leaders and critical partners like Bible League International, we have had the opportunity to cut our teeth and learn the basics of partnership. We've learned where we, as a local American megachurch, can provide help and add value to the ministries already underway in the nation of India. We have worked with our friends in India to pioneer a new model of holistic church planting that has led to more than one thousand church plants. In India, we first experienced church as movement and saw the power of *multiplication church planting.*

These experiences have led us to some additional values that are typically more characteristic of missional churches. Here are a few of the missional lessons we have learned from our involvement in multiplication church planting and incarnational mission:

- *Small and Reproducing.* The key to any missional success is keeping it small enough to be easily replicable. In India, for instance, we do not seek to directly reproduce Granger clones of five-thousand-member churches with massive facilities and several strata of highly trained professional staff. Rather, the average size of a faith community in India is probably twenty to fifty people, most likely meeting in a home or small, rented space. Meetings are led by a bivocational pastor who has been trained in a very modular, highly organic, coaching environment. Some of these churches do end up growing to megachurch dimensions (we have begun to see megachurches emerging in the past couple years), but most do not. Keeping them small and highly replicable allows them to grow quickly and spread virally.

- *Collaborative.* The mission of God is not accomplished merely in the religious sector of society or by a single local church. The most effective missional processes utilize a full gambit of partners to accomplish a core mission. This includes businesses, local communities, other church partners, outside organizations, NGOs and agencies, and even local and national governments. A kingdom vision includes players from every domain of society, and it requires collaboration across those domains.

- *Holistic.* The mission of God is holistic. In poverty-stricken environments, or when working with the sick, the marginalized, and the oppressed, an isolated message of "salvation after you die" radically reduces Jesus' intent. The mission of God requires both a verbal proclamation and a demonstration proclamation.

- *Meaningful Mobilization.* Missional churches must meaningfully mobilize every follower of Jesus in well-defined steps to draw them deeper into the mission of God in the world. Genuinely missional movements avoid the creation of specialized "commando Christians," an elite echelon of the body of Christ who are responsible for all the work that takes place outside the walls.
- *Disciple Making.* The strength of any missional movement rises and falls on its ability to make and reproduce disciples.

Despite our affirmation of these key missional values, we need to confess that there have been points of tension at times. We've probably seen this most evident in the way we structure the church and our ministry programs—our ecclesiology. To better explore this tension, we'd like to offer you a brief history lesson on the missional movement, something of a Missional 101 that will introduce you to the origins and growth of the missional idea.

In 1974, after forty years of missionary engagement in India, a man named Lesslie Newbigin returned to the West and noticed the evident decline of Christian influence in the surrounding culture. Newbigin began to think and dream about what it would take for the church in the West to reassume a place of influence in the surrounding culture, becoming a "missionary entity." At the time, the church-growth movement was getting started in the United States, a movement that would later be characterized by the attractional values we highlighted earlier. The focus of these attractional churches was mainly on methodology, looking for creative and fresh ways of "doing" church. By contrast, Newbigin and those influenced by his ideas were looking beyond methodology and recasting the conversation in terms of ecclesiology.

Newbigin emphasized that the mission of God precedes the identity of the church as an organized body: the church should be

neither the starting point nor the goal of mission. Newbigin emphasized that the church is taken up, swallowed up, and birthed out
of the *missio dei*, a Latin phrase referring to the mission of God.
Missional thinking saw the church as a decentralized movement
radiating outward into every culture, every pocket of people, and
every domain of society. In other words, the missional conversation
introduced a call for an ecclesiological reformation.

The potential for shaking the world with this new reformation
is every bit as big as the Reformation of the fifteenth and sixteenth
centuries, if not more so. Since the time of the Reformation, the
church has continued to express itself in less institutional forms. Yet
these more "movemental" forms of church have always been viewed
as the exception, not the norm for church structure. The missional
emphasis, first introduced by Newbigin and carried forward today
by voices like Alan Hirsch, tells us that the way forward for the
church is not going to be found in revising our methodology—simply
developing new programs—but in reframing our fundamental
understanding of the church—our ecclesiology. We need to hear
and live a different story about the church and reclaim an understanding of the church as a movement. We'll come back to this idea
in missional move 11.

The missional voices you hear today are saying that the attractional reformation in methodology is no longer sufficient to accomplish the mission of the church. Telling people to come and see is
not enough. We must also rethink our understanding of the church
and reclaim the biblical focus on the church as an organic movement outward to the world.

FROM MISSIONAL TO MOVEMENT

For the past several years, the people of Granger Community
Church have been dreaming about our future. What if the church
was everything Jesus wanted it to be? What would that look like?
We initiated a multilayered, open-source process with thousands

participating via web portal, focus groups, countless conversations, emails, letters, and even text messaging. While our lead team spent extensive time away in prayer and conversation, they didn't simply go up on the mountain and come back down with the vision. Instead, through countless conversations in smaller settings and hundreds of exchanges, we worked together to answer this simple and potent question, "What is the Spirit of God saying to the people of Granger Community Church?" The results were astounding, and they have been compiled into the next phase of planning for our journey together as a body of believers. We call it "Raising the BAR."

B: Be the Church. We want to see the number of people "being the church" in their neighborhoods, schools, cafes, and communities seven days a week outnumber the number of casual Christians coming to church services and sitting in our seats. The practical point of implementation for this value is an intensive training that launches missional communities around each of seven primary domains of society: health care, justice, government, education, religion, the arts, and family.

A: Activate the Campus. We will remodel our Granger campus and programs to serve the greater community, with Jesus at the center. The Granger campus will be opened to businesses, social groups, and the community at large and will be used as a community center for everything from high school formals to career fairs, college graduations, soccer practices, and pregnant mother exercise classes.

R: Reproduce at Every Level. Every follower of Jesus will be a reproducing follower of Jesus, and every church will be a reproducing church. It is our plan to launch three new multisites in our region, and to create more significant infrastructure for online campuses. We also plan to train and plant two thousand "essential churches" (small, viral, rapidly replicating groups within unreached pockets of people where ordinary people are trained to disciple fifteen to fifty people) locally, domestically, and internationally.

God did not develop laryngitis at the end of the first

Want to see the entire 2016 vision? Head to *missionalmoves.com*.

century. The Spirit is still leading, guiding, prompting, and yes, speaking to his people. When we listen together, we increase the chances of clarifying and amplifying what God is actually saying, while diminishing our own personal misperceptions that take us off course.

This new vision was birthed as hundreds of us listened to the wild and untamed Spirit of God. What is the Spirit saying? Together, we are Raising the BAR.

THE GENIUS OF THE *AND*

We've found that you can't be entirely faithful to some of the core incarnational values within attractional thinking and avoid being drawn into missional thinking—and vice versa. In other words, the contextualizing focus of attractional thinking is already embedded inside most missional churches, while all attractional churches with a healthy commitment to discipleship and mission will eventually seek a missional presence in their community. As we incarnate the gospel message in new contexts (missional), that will be profoundly attractive to people within those contexts (attractional).

We are convinced that the church in the West is on the verge of massive, category-shifting change. Our times require a different kind of church, an apostolic, reproducing movement where every person is living a mission-sent life, every church is a reproducing church.

Those incarnational values planted so long ago within our attractional approach are taking us to new places. For example, what was cultural relevance (attractional) is now becoming cultural embedment (missional). We're raising up a missionary presence for every subculture in our community. We are equipping and empowering our people—here at home—to go forth and live among the unique pocket of people they are called to reach with the same kind of adaptability and deep contextualization we learned in India. What if we plant the gospel in each subculture in our community? What if gifted-based ministry (attractional) that has been contained within the context of church programs, which we continue with strength, is now seen as a healthy step toward a movement of people infiltrating every domain of society as kingdom initiators, who realize most of their ministry must and will happen there (missional)?

We believe this new vision reflects the power of the *and*—attractional *and* missional. So let me summarize the power and the tension within the *and* by answering two closing questions:

1. Do we have to see attractional church (church as institution) and missional church (church as movement) as division, or can we see them as diversification? We believe the gospel can be faithfully expressed in both forms. When we have both forms, we are sturdy like a sumo wrestler, but we are also swift like a ninja. We want to be the sumo-ninja church, where we are both sturdy and swift.

What if we can actually be more responsive to the lead of the Holy Spirit by having both expressions playing together on purpose? Attractional and missional can exist in a healthy, dynamic relationship.

Institutions can set up a settlement where the pioneer movements have gone. Institutions can hold the ground, preserve the important gains of the pioneers, and in fact, become the supply chain, the distribution force, and most importantly, the launch pad for the pioneering movement out on the edges. That way, the movement's gains can deepen and expand the impact of the institution, while simultaneously the institution can preserve and empower the gains of the movement. That's what we've seen happen at the edges in Monroe Circle and India. Now this is becoming our approach everywhere.

At first, the civil rights movement was opposed by the institution of the United States government. But who is the primary entity that now preserves those gains through the Civil Rights Act and other legislation put into law? The US government.

In our own history, Monroe Circle Community Center started as a micromovement. The seed was the incarnational impulse inside two women — awakened by their deep engagement in an attractional church — who had their hearts broken on a mission trip. They decided a mission trip wasn't enough and embraced a missional lifestyle. More people joined the kingdom party without an organizational edict. It grew and blossomed. Then the institution of Granger Community Church said, "Let's hold this ground, let's fund this movement, let's empower what's happening here so it's sustainable and brings lasting benefit." We believe that God's Spirit empowers and enlivens both expressions of church.

You'll have to decide what you think.

2. *Are attractional and missional mutually exclusive, or can the two come together?* Let's go back to the beginning. What started this whole story? The Granger story started as a missional impulse inside of Mark and Sheila Beeson. When they moved to Granger to start a mission outpost, that move was missional in its impulse — the missional heartbeat of God inside of Mark and Sheila. That same missional heartbeat was the rhythm we danced to at Monroe Circle and India, as megachurch went missional locally and globally. That missional impulse has been beating in this church for twenty-five years. That missional EKG looks like cross-stitching, woven through our entire history, weaving missional and attractional together. Not only can the two come together, but we're convinced that these two can dance together and make beautiful kingdom music.

Simultaneously, we recognize the constant dynamic tension between missional and attractional. We believe that God enlivens church as institution, but church as movement is both our biblical origin and our prophetic future. We recognize that the "come and see" model has extra weight we have to jettison. What needs to change? Where do attractional and missional contradict each other? Let me be brutally honest.

For years, the weekend services have been the organizing factor of our church. We've seen the unintended consequences of that and it has broken our hearts. Too many equate evangelism with an invitation to a service where a professional pastor can do the work for you. Too many people have developed a codependent relationship with the weekend and feel unable to convey God's story in their own voice in their own context. Too many have let a great weekend experience become a commodity that provides the weekly shot in the arm they need, while remaining mostly passive in their own development as a disciple of Jesus. Default mode in the attractional world often means we've spent so much time creating great environments for corporate shepherding of the masses, that we have not put the requisite energy needed into making disciples who can make disciples. The Reveal Survey by Willow Creek confirmed that we were not alone. Thousands of churches find themselves in the very same place. The new normal for Granger means that any corporate environments must exist for the purpose of initiating, enhancing, and amplifying disciple making.

By 2016, we hope the weekend will no longer be a gathering of individuals and families who see themselves as simply going to church. By 2016, we want the weekend to be the gathering of little platoons of people—groups of twenty to fifty—who are doing life together all week, being the church in their neighborhood, workplace, and community through a missional community. Most of the experience of "church" in the early church happened in these smaller households where life-on-life, obedience-based discipleship happened on a daily basis and strengthened every follower of Jesus to live flat-out on mission in all of life, despite the threat of persecution or martyrdom. By 2016, our new organizing factor will be these small, reproducing missional communities that are embedded in every neighborhood, workplace, and campus in our community.

Does that mean the weekend services will diminish or become optional? Does that mean weekends will be for insider meetings and that being attractional will come to an end? No way. In our view, that would be the opposite of missional. We're still radically committed to an attractional approach on the weekend. These vibrant gatherings fulfill a unique role of celebration, motivation, vision casting, and momentum building for the movement. More and more, we see the weekend as the gathering space for the scattered church.

Like the early church, the larger gatherings will be the overflow, accumulation, and gathering space for hundreds of missional communities. These times of gathering will continue to powerfully shape our identity with every smaller expression of church—fueling their connection to the larger Granger movement. We've been scattered on mission; now we gather to lock arms, celebrate, and encourage. But let me ask: What could be more attractive? Imagine all that diversity being unified in worship for the glory of Jesus Christ, the only one big enough to bring us all together. In that place, it becomes a foretaste of the maximum glory we will know when every tribe is gathered together in the new heaven and new earth.

In addition, we still live in a culture where the right next step for millions of unchurched people is attending a weekend service. Listen, as powerful and essential as missional communities are, for huge numbers of people they will not be the right first connection for them to find their way into the life of the church. The attractional weekend services continue to give people a safe place to investigate and walk around the edges before they move further in or make any commitments.

Let's be honest: having the institutional connection is just more culturally acceptable to many people. Believe it or not, that means it's incarnational to offer attractional weekend service!

I believe this is especially true for communities with high numbers of dechurched people like we have in our region, which lies within the shadow of the Roman Catholic presence of Notre Dame. Dechurched people are those who may have experienced church, but have not experienced a vital faith connection with Jesus. Dechurched people are those who may have experienced church, but were turned off and haven't been back for a long time.

Just this last week, I bumped into a gentleman at the grocery story who said, "I grew up in the Catholic church. When I became an adult, I drifted away. God mattered to me, but church actually didn't seem to help me connect with God. I couldn't see how it was relevant to my life. A friend invited me to come to a weekend service here at GCC, and I can't describe to you the impact the services have had on my life. I'm a completely different person because the weekends helped me connect with God in a way that made sense to my everyday life." At that point, he was tearing up and his body was shaking.

I can't tell you how many times I have heard similar stories from the dechurched. For dechurched people, an attractional service provides a touch point with their past that is legitimate enough to start with. Many dechurched people, although they were turned off by institutional church, still want the credibility of institutional church that was affirmed as part of their upbringing.

Also, Americans are accustomed to excellence in every area of life. Our corporate gatherings allow a place to express the excellence in arts, teaching, and environment that not only is our God worthy of but people in our culture are actually longing for. Again, that sounds incarnational to me. We fully expect that not only will we grow through missional communities, but through the weekend services.

There it is again ... the genius of the *and*.

In the last section, "Decentralized Shift: The People of God On Mission," we'll unpack five missional moves that are helping GCC jump the curve, realizing the return of the movement. We'll dive into launching missional communities, engaging the domains of society on mission, structuring for "movemental" expression, and much more.

We're at the end of a twenty-five-year run at Granger, but as you can tell, we're really just at the beginning. Recently Mark said, "We're starting the church all over again. I feel like I did twenty-five years ago when Sheila and I risked it all to plant a mission outpost in Granger, except now our start-up group includes another five thousand people!"

On a personal note, when I started with Mark twenty years ago, I (Rob) thought megachurch was the summit. But once we got there, we realized, "Oh brother, this is only base camp. The summit Jesus is calling us to is so much higher."

Everyone on our team will tell you, we go back and forth between unbelievable excitement and flat-out fear — a holy fear. When we look at this vision, we have this radical, completely, absolute, total dependency on the lordship of Jesus and the power of the Holy Spirit. I'm thinking that's a good thing. A really good thing.

Churches that are truly committed to the mission of God will see value in appropriating insights from both the missional and attractional — transcending the false dichotomy for an integrated approach. That is the beauty and genius in the *and*.

Chapter 5

FROM THE CENTER TO THE MARGINS
Missional Move 5

We both grew up watching reruns of *The Beverly Hillbillies*, a quirky old show from the 1960s about a group of backwoods bumpkins who strike oil on their property and suddenly move from the squalor of the Appalachian wilderness to the opulence of Beverly Hills, California. For those of you who have seen or remember the show, it always started with the same catchy theme song and tells the story of how a poor mountain family became wealthier than an Arabian sultan and moved from their life of poverty to one of wealth and pleasure.

At a spiritual level, this is also the story of every follower of Jesus. We're all Beverly hillbillies! Even if we are living at the apex of material wealth, in our spiritual brokenness and guilt before God, we are all poor and needy. We can "barely keep our family fed." One day, we find Jesus and experience a miracle of grace. Jesus calls to us, and it is like striking a gold mine or finding an oil reservoir. Black gold! Texas tea! He is all of the things we have hoped for and dreamed of. He provides us with a wealth of hope and love and life and forgiveness. In Jesus, we begin to experience an affluence of purpose and meaning that we had never known before.

What do we typically do with this newfound treasure? Why, move to Beverly Hills, of course! We get the heck out of Dodge and move to a place where that new spiritual affluence can take us as far as we can get from the poverty we once knew. We find new friends, perhaps a new neighborhood, get new clothes, new music, new schools, and maybe even new jobs. At first, we feel a little odd in our new surroundings. But soon we learn to adapt, and within a generation, the "hillbilly" is all but gone. And what about our poor "kin" still left in Appalachia? After a short period of time, they are all but forgotten. After all, this isn't a show about what happens when Jed and Ma and Jethro and Ellie Mae stay in Appalachia and use their newfound wealth to transform the lives of the people around them. Life is just "better in Beverly."

Unfortunately, followers of Christ are often like the hillbillies. We tend to use our newfound hope and status to better our own condition, rather than using it to serve those in great need around us. We aren't interested in heading back into the mountains to reach those living in darkness. Rather than being propelled by the top-line blessing to fulfill our bottom-line responsibility, we'd rather stay safe inside our mansion sanctuaries.

Recently, I (Jack) met with a crisis of faith that called into question my own "move to Beverly." It wasn't a crisis of belief. I wasn't questioning if God exists or if Jesus is really the Savior of the world. Rather, my crisis of faith was wondering if God is at work among the poor, the oppressed, the hungry, the sick, the widows, and the orphans in a unique way. In short, is there a greater openness to the work of God among the people at the fringes and the margins of society than among those of us in more materially affluent contexts? While I was initially tempted to dismiss this question, the opportunities I've been given to serve, both home and abroad, would not let the question lie dormant. I couldn't help but notice a stark contrast between my work among affluent American Christians and the work I've done with people who have little or nothing. In fact, the transformation I'd seen in these contexts seemed to outscale, in a profound way, what is happening among those of us who have ... well ... everything we need. Why is that? And if it is true, what are we supposed to do about it?

AN INCONVENIENT TRUTH ... BUT WITHOUT THE GLOBAL WARMING

When we turn to the pages of Scripture, it appears that God does indeed have a soft spot for those living on the margins. God's desire is that "none should perish" and that all might have an opportunity to experience his shalom in their lives, and he is always at work among the broken, the lost, the hungry, the sick, and the oppressed. God is a God on a mission, and he is always going to be at work where his mission is not yet accomplished, and that typically involves bringing healing to those who are hurting, freedom to those in bondage, and hope to those who are discouraged. If we are content accepting his blessing but have no desire to change our lives in response to that blessing, we miss the point of the blessing in the first place. Though God freely gives grace beyond our understanding, he seems to have little tolerance for those who hoard his blessings for themselves.

To be clear, when we suggest that God is at work among the poor and broken and needy of this world in a special way, we want to immediately add that we're *all* broken and poor and needy in some fashion. Material poverty may lead to greater dependence and receptivity to assistance, but it's no guarantee that a person will bow their knee to God. At the same time, though a person may have wealth and riches, they must first come to acknowledge their spiritual poverty to experience the grace of God. The truth is that we're all poor in one way or another. We all have fallen short of

God's mark for shalom in our lives, and we all need God's gracious assistance to deliver us.[1]

In other words, everybody is poor. We may be able to delude ourselves by believing that we are financially secure, keeping up with the Joneses, and therefore "don't need God," but exposure to those who live at the margins often reveals other forms of poverty in our lives. Many of the people from our church who have traveled to India have commented on the relational wealth that our friends in that country possess, even in the midst of their material poverty. Our Indian friends express generosity, giving out of their destitution rather than their excess. They have learned to be joyful, even with few possessions, and they are blessed with the gift of authentic relationships because they have learned to depend on one another. When we debrief our teams, they often begin to share a sense of nakedness after their experience. Like a bad adolescent dream of walking into class and then realizing that they are wearing only their underwear, most of our team members become aware—not only of what they have that others do not—but also of what they are missing in their lives.

There are many ways of defining wealth and poverty. For instance, in India, an entire village functions like an extended family. You are not just a neighbor who gets an occasional wave. You are a brother, sister, aunt, mother, father to every child and person in the village. Every home is your home. In our experience, this is far from the norm in our American context. Consider how long it would take for us as Americans to build that kind of community, to experience the kind of trust and intimacy that these people have each day, in our own neighborhoods and towns. Years? Perhaps decades? Yes, America and the American church is rich in material resources. But in many other ways, we are naked and poor, in need of help.

We all have ways in which we are poor. But the opposite is true, as well. In some way, as a follower of Christ, each one of us is rich.

In Christ, God has made you rich. In some area of your life, you are affluent, regardless of your age, race, creed, or position. In fact, there is someone else in your life right now who needs the influence of your affluence. Your riches can be used to help alleviate their poverty. At the same time, in some area of your life, you are poor. You lack knowledge, experience, understanding, skill, and perspective. You are desperately in need of help.

Knowing where I am rich and where I am poor is sacred knowledge, something that only God's Spirit can reveal to me. That sacred knowledge is the only way to avoid the trap of arrogance and pride. This is what Paul refers to in Romans 12:3 when he says, "For by the grace given me I say to every one of you: Do not think of yourself more highly than you ought, but rather think of yourself with sober judgment, in accordance with the measure of faith God has given you" (NIV 1984).

Paul tells us that we have all been given a measure of faith through the grace of God. There are ways in which we are lacking in faith, and we need others to serve us and help us. And there are ways in which God wants to use us to be a blessing to others. Everybody is poor. Everybody is rich.

FLUENCY: IT'S NOT JUST ABOUT THE WORDS YOU USE

Typically, those who possess material wealth approach other communities they perceive to be in material poverty with the notion that those communities have no wealth of their own from which to benefit. Thus the wealthy community ignorantly assumes it is the benevolent distributor of all that the receiver community needs. For true transformation to occur, however, the "wealthy" must realize that they too must and will be changed as they give of themselves to others. Our friend Joel Holm calls this idea "fluency" (fig. 5.1).

Figure 5.1

Fluency is like a geyser (think Old Faithful at Yellowstone). When water, located beneath the surface and superheated by magma, turns to steam, it joins with other water as it rises through the earth's crust, finally jettisoning forth in an explosion of power and moisture. We would suggest that the kingdom of God is like a geyser. As our lives are heated up by the power of God's Spirit, it creates energy that is forced outward. To help explain this idea, we want to introduce you to four key words: affluence, influence, confluence, and effluence.

Affluence. One way of talking about wealth is by referring to it as affluence. Affluence literally means "flow to." Our affluence or wealth is what we have been given as a result of God's kingdom work in our lives. It's God's blessing, and as we stated earlier, everyone who belongs to Christ is rich in some way. We have been blessed with these riches so that we might share them with those in need.

Affluence → Influence. Influence is another helpful word that literally means "flow in." Our influence is what flows out of us, from our lives into the lives of others. It can affect them either positively or negatively. In God's kingdom, our influence results from our affluence. We can offer only what we have already been given. But as we give, our influence grows. Affluence that is hoarded has no influence. But when affluence is used to engage in the mission of God in the world, for kingdom purposes, it "flows into" others.

Affluence → Influence → Confluence. When our influence is joined to the affluence and influence of another culture, it gains even more power and momentum, creating confluence. Confluence literally means to "flow with and together." When we experience confluence, we are mutually interdependent with one another, blending our relative wealth and poverty to achieve strength and power that none of us possesses alone.

Affluence → Influence → Confluence → Effluence. As the work of God in and through us, meeting one another's needs with our own resources, picks up speed over time, God causes this amazing work to burst forth in a way that all can see. This is called effluence. Effluence means literally to "flow out"—it is the explosive overflow of transformation and beauty that is the end result of the fluency process. The water falls back to the ground, where it recycles in a continual process of fluency that redeems both cultures.

When you enter into my poverty with your riches and I enter into your poverty with my riches, we are all transformed. Everyone benefits when we recognize our own poverty, bring the best of who we are and what we are into the mix of God's work in the world, and let the forward momentum of that transformative engine bring the entire world into a state of shalom with its Creator.

THE TRANSFORMATION CYCLE

Recognizing both my poverty and my wealth as gifts from God has helped me to be drawn into what God is doing all around me.

When we bring our blessing (our riches) to people living in need, we find that God is ready to use what we have to bless others. And as we bring our wealth, our own poverty is exposed. We see where we are insufficient to fix problems, where we ourselves need help and assistance from others. In this process, we experience a refinement of God's blessing, as God changes us, molds us, lifts us up, and fills our cups again. The more we are drawn in to serve others with our wealth, the more we pour ourselves out, exposing our poverty. And as we pour ourselves out, we find that we are filled back up. This is the process that God uses to change us and draw us into his mission. We call this process the "transformation cycle" (fig. 5.2). By its cyclical action, it generates both the power and the momentum to transform our lives and our communities. It begins with the understanding that we have been blessed by the saving grace of our Lord and Savior, Jesus. He has given us what this sin-sick world needs—forgiveness of sins and the empowering presence of the Spirit. Within us resides the very power that raised Jesus from the grave and gave him the name that is above every name!

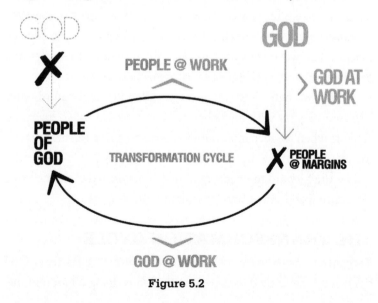

Figure 5.2

The problem is that many of us just stay right there. We avoid people with needs, those living on the margins. Our tank is full, but the key isn't in the ignition and the pedal is not being pressed down to the metal. Our friend Raj, who serves with us in southern India, calls this state "Christians asleep in the love of God." There is a human tendency to fall asleep in the peace that provides. In this state, we are unconscious of the world around us. The problem is that if you perpetually sleep, you eventually lapse into a coma. But that is not God's plan for us. Instead, we must learn to "wake up" and join God in his work at the margins, pouring ourselves out for the sake of others. As we serve others, we exhaust our resources and must return to "sleep" again, relying upon the gracious empowerment of God's Spirit. As we sleep, we are refreshed and awaken again to join God in his work, this time with renewed energy. This can be a healthy process that strengthens us and disciplines us to rely upon God and to serve others.

WEALTH IN THE HARD-TO-REACH PLACES

In the West, Christians typically live in relative comfort and ease. We do not typically see or experience God meeting our material needs in extraordinary ways. Rather, we find him when we follow him to places that cost us something, when we are asked to sacrifice something or called to spend our time and energy doing something that is of little direct benefit to ourselves. Paradoxically, when we embrace the impossible task, the difficult person, or the calling that calls us to sacrifice, we discover the true wealth available to us in God's kingdom.

Gold is valuable because it is hard to find. It occurs in hard-to-reach places. Typically, things become more valuable when they are available only in limited quantities or they are difficult to acquire. We believe that in some mysterious way, the best way for us to uncover and discover the wealth we so desire in our lives—the gold of God's kingdom—is to pour ourselves out to meet the poverty of others. We find God's wealth when we engage those in need.

Author and church planter/trainer Neil Cole comments in his book *Organic Church* that:

> It is not that smart, moral, and wealthy people do not come to Christ and bear fruit; the point is that "not many" will respond from these sectors. God loves all people, but there will be fewer who respond in these domains of culture than from [those at the margins of society]. This is just a true fact that statistics and the Scriptures confirm. If you are called to a wealthy, educated segment of the population, God is pleased and will bless your ministry, but you will not see as many come to Christ as those who work with the marginalized and the poor segments of the population. You will be hard-pressed to find a church planting movement started among the wealthy, educated people. But it is easy to find them among poor, working-class people.[2]

Several years ago, I was in Cambodia visiting church planters who were operating in the remote regions of the country. We approached a small structure, and I saw some of the most joyful but bedraggled people I have ever seen lifting up their hands and praising God with the full sound of their voices. As I scanned the fifty or so faces, I saw many who looked hungry, a few who were obviously sick, and most who were thin and wasted from the results of both. A little girl who sat on the lap of a woman looked up at me with curious eyes. As I watched her, I noticed that while she had legs, she could not walk due to muscle atrophy caused by chronic malnutrition.

I turned to my friend Bob, who has helped to build the infrastructure necessary to train the church planters in the network, and asked him about the village. Bob explained the story of the village to me. He said, "These people were the remaining descendants of the Khmer Rouge, the people who perpetrated the horrific genocidal massacre within the country in the 1970s under the regime of Pol Pot. This regime destroyed families, murdered more than

30 percent of the country's inhabitants, destroyed all the industry, and effectively took the country back to the Stone Age. When the North Vietnamese Army chased the Khmer Rouge out, most of them fled to the rugged hill country where we are standing. The environments were so remote and extreme that most people seeking retribution against them were content to leave them there to die."

As I looked over the little group with a new understanding of their identity, I asked Bob about the pastor who was leading worship in their midst. Bob smiled and said, "Most of this pastor's family was murdered by the Khmer Rouge. Initially, he hated them, but after he came to Jesus, God laid a burden for them upon his heart. After receiving church-planter training, this man journeyed the many miles into the rugged and remote interior of the country and sought out this village. He has been planting a church here for the past six months. Already fifty to seventy-five people have decided to follow Jesus as a result of his ministry."

I looked again over the huddled band of people and watched them for a few moments. The wives, brothers, sisters, and children of murderers turned fugitives, some of them probably former Khmer Rouge themselves, were now sitting together singing praises to God. The church was being led by a man who just forty years ago would have been shot and dumped into a swamp with countless other bodies. These people were now living at the margins, and yet here was Jesus in their midst, offering them hope, forgiveness, relationship, love, and life.

I was also struck to realize that these people were now *my* brothers and my sisters, my mothers and *my* fathers. Visiting the margins to share what I had—knowledge that could help better equip their leaders—I found a treasure from God, a fresh realization of his amazing grace and the transforming power of the unity we have in Christ. It was a profound example of the transformation cycle at work in my own soul, as I poured out what I had been given and in the process was filled back up again.

Hopefully you can already sense that these paradigm shifts we are presenting will require a whole new way of living out your mission as a local church. Standard operating procedure will not get the job done. That's why, with the foundation of the *why* firmly laid, it's now time for us to move into the *how*.

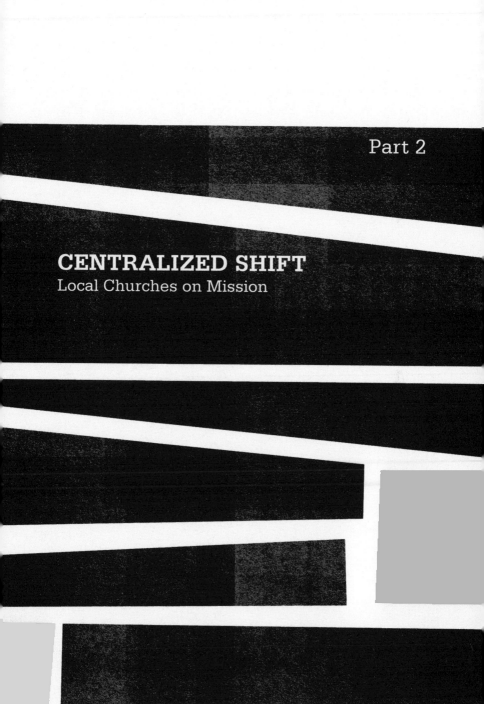

Part 2

CENTRALIZED SHIFT
Local Churches on Mission

At this point, we hope you have done some heavy thinking about your own core assumptions. Now we move from paradigm to pragmatics. This next section will provide a map for local churches and new church plants to be unleashed on mission, both locally and globally.

In the first section, we needed to expand, finding our way into a bigger story. In this section, expansion would probably end up killing us. Most churches are already doing too much. Don't consider these missional moves as something for you to layer on to what you are already doing. In this section, it's time to shift.

Centralized Shift

6. From Top Down to Bottom Up
7. From Diffused to Focused
8. From Transactional to Transformational Partnerships
9. From Relief to Development
10. From Professionals to Full Participation

Chapter 6

FROM TOP DOWN TO BOTTOM UP
Missional Move 6

Having grown up in the cocoon of suburban comfort, I (Rob) had never seen anything like the scene in front of me. From where I stood, I could see a throbbing mass of over one million displaced Sudanese living in a ring around the capital city of Khartoum. It was a swirling eddy powered by civil war, genocide, religious persecution, abject poverty, life-threatening illness, and dignity-stealing terror.

My host pulled me by the arm, moving me toward a tiny hut made out of bricks of sun-dried mud. Inside I was introduced to a man named George and his brother, Joseph. Eighteen months before my arrival in Sudan, the violence of war had decimated much of the nation. George and countless others had run for their lives, hoping to find refuge in the capital. Instead, George found debilitating disease.

Shortly after George had arrived in the refugee camp, he began to lose function on the right side of his body. With no doctor or health facilities available, his diagnosis remained a mystery and no treatments were available. George soon found himself paralyzed, spending his days on a cot with a hole cut for his buttocks. Each day, the excrement piled up beneath him and the flies swarmed around him. After I listened to George recount his story, he did not ask me for money or medicine. Nor did he ask me to help him get out of this hell on earth. He simply said, "Will you lay hands on me and pray?" Just prayer.

My first thought, selfishly, was of myself. *Lay hands? No way. Whatever he has, I'm going to get it for sure if I touch him.* Mother Teresa I am not. I immediately sensed my selfishness and was ashamed at my hesitance. Yet even as I overcame my initial reluctance, I was immediately overcome by doubts. What effect could my prayer have on this man? The problems that George faced were overwhelming to me. Still, I reached out to put my hand upon this man, touching his wasted shoulder, and I prayed for him. And as I prayed, I had a clear sense that I wasn't just touching a sick, forgotten refugee. In some way, I sensed Jesus touching me. As the words of my prayer poured out of my mouth, the gentle nudge of the Spirit spoke to my heart: "Look at the size and scale of the problems and need around you. I asked you for one small intervention. Yet you withhold it. Why?"

George (left) and his brother Joseph

Jesus has a way of asking irritating questions like that. But it was a good question. Why would I withhold such a small intervention?

Ever since that moment, I've thought about that question and how the "smallness" of the intervention I was making seemed ridiculous compared to the "bigness" of the problems. My intervention seemed useless when compared to the complex systems that created the poverty and atrocity in the first place. Have you ever felt that way? Have you ever looked at the problems and wondered, "What difference can I make against that?"

The truth is that we live in a world full of big problems. There is pollution that chokes the life from our world, the growing gap between the haves and have-nots, and an astronomical number of people who don't have clean water, sanitation, basic health care, safe housing, or education. And there are the spiritual challenges we face—the large numbers of people who have yet to even hear the name of Jesus. The problems of this world can seem overwhelming. And these are not just problems "out there." They are right here inside our own communities. They are everywhere, and they mean life or death for the billions who walk the planet today, every one a person who matters to God.

TOP DOWN: A BIG PROBLEM REQUIRES A BIG SOLUTION

So how do we respond? What should our churches be doing to address these problems? Most of the time, we look for Goliath-sized answers to Goliath-sized problems. We see a global giant like HIV/AIDS striding onto the battlefield. It mocks us, and we start looking for the biggest, baddest organization, agency, government system, program, or process we can find to take up the sword and charge out to meet it. And when we find a solution like this, we cheer it on without ever having to unsheathe our own sword and charge into the battle. We trust the experts, the professional warriors who have trained their entire lives for this fight. We shrug our shoulders, resigned to the fact that we're just a farmer in the ranks, three rows back with a rusty sickle. Let Bono handle the problem. Or Bill Gates. Or Warren Buffet. Or the expert economists. Or our government leaders. Or those large aid organizations. Surely, they have answers. They must know how to solve these problems. Don't they?

While organizations and programs can be helpful, when we look at the pattern of God's work throughout Scripture, we see that God seldom confronts a Goliath with another Goliath. Instead, he uses shepherd boys like David. He sends cowards like Gideon to lead his people. He enters history as a poor carpenter's son. God uses the small and powerless to uproot the powerful and defeat the giants. While influence and power can certainly be used in ways that honor God, you don't have to have great influence and means to make a kingdom-sized difference. God takes small acts of faith and transforms them into world-changing movements.

BOTTOM UP: A BIG PROBLEM REQUIRES A SMALL SOLUTION

According to Jesus, a kingdom mindset turns our natural ways of solving problems upside down. This means that a good way to address big problems is to start by thinking small. When it comes to kingdom transformation, Jesus uses the imagery of things like seeds and yeast—things that are small, organic, and reproducing. "He told them another parable: 'The kingdom of heaven is like a mustard seed, which a man took and planted in his field. Though it is the *smallest of all your seeds*, yet when it grows, it is the largest of garden plants and becomes a tree, so that the birds come and perch in its branches'" (Matt. 13:31–32, emphasis added).

Instead of giving us big solutions engineered to trickle top-down from the echelons of the wealthy and powerful, Jesus' approach is countercultural—a bottom-up perspective.

Over and over again, Jesus brings us back to the beauty of small interventions: a towel and a basin, a cup of cold water, a little bit of fish and a few loaves, the smallest seed and a little bit of leaven. This affirms that the little things we do in faith can have tremendous value. Jesus says, "A little leaven is enough. Trust me." In other words, God will take and use bottom-up, intentional, strategic, small interventions to make a huge impact. Just like it takes thousands of little pockets of carbon dioxide to elevate a piece of dough, it takes thousands of little, intentional, strategic interventions to elevate a life or a community in a way that makes a noticeable difference in the world.

Bottom-up approaches require a reversal of thinking because they are often radically different from standard operating procedure. Henry Blackaby writes, "Even the casual or uninformed reader of the Bible can see God's ways ... are radically different from people's. God uses kingdom methods to accomplish kingdom purposes. God reveals his ways to us because they are the only means to accomplishing his purposes. We must do God's work God's way."[1]

A couple of years ago, I (Jack) had a discussion with my then nine-year-old son, Elijah, about how the world's problems tend to be very much like the Death Star in the movie *Star Wars*. The problems seem massive and powerful enough to destroy our entire planet. So how does the rebel army finally take down the Death Star? Do they build a powerful version of their own to attack it? No. Instead, they find the weakness in the Death Star and launch a massive counteroffensive of one-manned fighters who fly through the superstructure, evading the defenses, depending on maneuverability, speed, and coordinated swarms of squadrons to finally deal a deathblow to the empire's ultimate weapon. Carrying the image into our conversation, I told my son, "Jesus came to train fleets of X-wing pilots to take down the Death Stars of our day." He understood the point: Jesus uses the big power of small things.

TOP DOWN VERSUS BOTTOM UP

There are several differences between a top-down and a bottom-up approach to solving problems.

Starting Organizationally versus Starting Relationally

When most churches look for ways to act locally and globally outside their four walls, they start by searching for organizations to work with. As church leaders with limited time and resources, we understand why this is the intuitive response. We want to make sure our small interventions are making the biggest impact possible, so it seems to make sense to begin with the professionals. If our people want to get involved, they can get in the slipstream of the pros who know what they are doing by volunteering or joining a short-term mission team. And organizational support is certainly helpful. We need the experience and expertise that they bring to the table. For example, I wouldn't presume to walk into an operating room where a group of surgeons are doing brain surgery and say, "Hey, boys, let me have a go at it! I don't know what I'm doing, but I'm sure if I poke around enough, I'll eventually figure it out!"

But we must also remember that when God sent his Son to change the course of human history, he did it by becoming one of us, living in our world, eating our food, and experiencing our pain as a real person. God himself came in Jesus; he didn't send an organization on his behalf. He came offering the infinitely rich treasure of the Trinity, the riches of his eternal relationships. And relationships are the means of Jesus' revolution. While top-down changes start with organizations and institutions, a bottom-up approach starts with existing relationships in your community. Certainly, we continue to partner and work with organizations, both locally and globally. We just don't start there. We begin with ministry approaches that focus on relationships with people and then establish organizational partnerships that enhance existing relationships. Adopting an off-the-shelf approach that relies on organization to deliver the real impact circumvents the discipleship process that Jesus intends. Local churches that begin with organizations, rather than relationships, risk:

- *Running programs rather than relating to people.* If you start with the organization, you run the risk of implementing their programs regardless of need and without the buy-in of the community itself. When we substitute programs for relationships, we have lost our incarnational moorings.

- *Reinforcing the "You're a number, not a person" mindset.* Organizations abound, and people in marginalized communities are smart. They know that funding is tied to metrics and so, as a result, tend to treat organizations as "systems to be used." They perceive that the system uses them to get funding, and in return, they get a tangible benefit (i.e., food, water, etc.). As a result, they say, "I'm a number, not a person to them. So I will use the system to get whatever I can from it. I can abuse a system and not feel bad about it." This inadvertently creates a codependent relationship. When you start with relationships, you are seen as a person, someone who knows and cares about the problems in the community.

- *Remaining blind.* Relationships are far more accurate than organizational forms and processes for troubleshooting particular community problems. When something is working well, and when it's not, people will typically share it with their friends sooner than they will tell a faceless organization. Information is typically more accurate when it is reported through the conduit of relationships rather than given to organizational personnel who may not have a relational connection to the person sharing the information.

Start Organizationally: An identified problem requires a proven organizational expert with a proven track record for success in delivering a given initiative in a particular context. Values are guaranteed impact and efficiency with security in expertise. "Ask the Experts."	**Start Relationally:** An identified problem requires an intimate understanding of the people involved, their individual culture, and identifiable relationships with people in that context. Values are trust, communication, and mutual community. "Ask the People."

EnterMission Story // Starting Relationally and Learning to Listen
Paul Worth, Senior Pastor
Relevant Church, EnterMission Hub, Tampa, Florida

Relevant Church is a six-year-old church plant in the heart of Ybor City, which is the club district of Tampa. From day one, they have perceived themselves as missionaries to the mixed crowd that populates their neighborhood, including everyone from successful young professionals to the homeless, from the gay and transgender community to the inner-city at-risk families trapped in generational poverty. During the first three years, they've gained growing influence on the twenty-somethings within Ybor through their attractional expression, but within just a few blocks of where their facilities are located in the heart of the club district, you'll find Tampa Park, a forgotten housing project, and a forgotten elementary school called Booker T. Washington. Paul says, "When I say forgotten, we mean it. Booker T. is the only F-rated school in our entire county."

Paul continues, "It all started in the heart of one of our church elders, Tim, who felt burdened to walk Tampa Park every Sunday morning before service. As he prayed, he had this growing sense God was calling us beyond our 'Jerusalem'—the folks we were reaching on the weekends—into our 'Judea' and 'Samaria.' Our movement on mission would begin in our own back yard. Due to our exposure to the missional moves, we had been prepared to start small and with a laser focus."

As a next step, they met with the director of housing at Tampa Park. The director expressed skepticism and said point-blank, "Churches have tried working down here before. They just end up leaving. They come and do enough so they feel better about themselves, and then they leave."

Paul said, "We're not here with a big agenda about what we want to do. What is it that the people of this community already have in their hearts and hands to make happen? How can we help with that?" This approach, based on the ideas behind transformational partnership, took the director by surprise.

Over the coming months, the people of Relevant were invited by the people of Tampa Park and Booker T. Washington into a series of community events like a community field day, beautification projects in Tampa Park, and a back-to-school event. During one of those events, Paul met an elderly grandmother who was raising several of her grandchildren. She commented on their activity in the community and asked, "Why?" Paul explained, "Our church gathers in Ybor City, just down the street." Her response: "What took you so long to show up?" Paul says, "That was my wake-up call. I think there are countless under-resourced communities surrounded by churches that haven't shown up. Where is the church?"

Over the last two years, that friendship has blossomed. More than seventy-five kids from the school are now mentored and tutored one-on-one by the people of Relevant. The schoolteachers are encouraged regularly with care packages and special events just for them. A choir of Booker T. Washington kids now sing at Relevant's Easter celebration. Numerous families have been baptized. This year Booker T. Washington jumped from the F-grade to a C-grade status, receiving "The Most Improved School" award from the county. This year Relevant is helping the school reinstitute academics, arts, and athletics. Their goal is to put the A's back into the community. That's a kingdom breakthrough!

Expecting Perfection versus Embracing Experiments

Experimenting is expensive and painful, and so we often want to eliminate it from the process of discovering what works best in a given environment. It's tempting to just "go to the experts" and ask them for a packaged program that can be delivered with precision, perfection, and predictability. But here's the reality: even those packages are seldom predictable, precise, or truly perfect—if you stay on the ground long enough to watch the aftermath.

A bottom-up experimenting approach creates a laboratory environment for the development of people and the building of character. The bottom line isn't just measurable results on the field. The bottom line must also include the transformation of people. The permission-to-fail, experimenting approach fosters avid learning, commitment, ownership, creativity, innovation, assessment, and reassessment inside both the people who go to serve and those who are being served. Both parties begin to perceive each other as lab partners: "We can only figure this out together." We're not saying "be stupid" or "reinvent the wheel" or "don't gather as much information as you can before you try something," but rather that after you've done all that you can to evaluate and prepare, don't be afraid to try, or even to try and fail.

We learned this the hard way in a small community in India called Pudu. In this tiny village, families struggled with all sorts of water-borne illnesses as they drank from an infected cistern. At first glance, we thought, "Aha! Let's get some clean water in here!" That was the easy part—identifying the problem. The longer and more complicated story is that we spent more than $20,000 on initiatives aimed at providing what was supposed to be a low-cost, low-tech, point-of-use system to give clean water to each home. Instead, we purchased an opportunity to learn that an easy solution to the complete reengineering of a community's water and sanitation process simply doesn't exist. Our efforts were strangely similar to that old song about the old woman who swallowed a fly; one problem was always tagged, chased, or somehow interconnected with another. Finally, we realized that any initiative in rural India that tries to provide clean water is at minimum a long-term, fifteen-step process. When potential partners claim that they can deliver "clean water" but focus only on one or two of the steps needed, we chuckle.

This example, however, is not presented as a failure. Far from it! Instead, we view it as a success because we learned critical lessons about what is involved in community water, sanitation, consensus building, and the belief structures of the people we were serving. That $20,000 worth of failure has saved us ten times that amount by teaching us valuable lessons that have kept us from repeating basic errors in other environments.

A top-down approach expects perfection and looks for guaranteed results. But a bottom-up approach is more flexible, learning through trial and error how to best serve the community. It embraces failure as an opportunity to learn.

Expect Perfection: Results are guaranteed based on highly defined metrics such as number of houses built, number of mothers cared for, number of books distributed. There is little margin for experimentation and trial and error. "Failure is not an option!"	**Embrace Experiments:** A "laboratory" methodology is critical, and trial-and-error are necessary evolutions to determine what best works in a given context or community. "Failure is a necessary part of success!"

Need-Based versus Asset-Based

Top-down vision sees a need. A bottom-up perspective, however, sees an asset (fig. 6.1). Our natural tendency is to look at the poor in terms of their neediness, while ignoring their wealth. But the poor often have incredible assets. An asset-based approach to transformation assumes that by God's grace the seeds necessary for a community's transformation already exist within that community at some level. There will always be strategic ways to leverage the strengths that a church partner can bring to a community, but that should only happen after the "gold" has been mined from within the community.

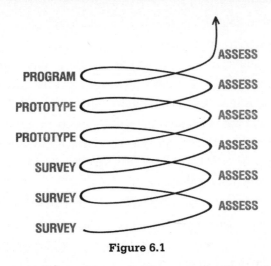

Figure 6.1

Before initiating programs in downtown South Bend, we were able to do a series of house-to-house surveys, community forums, and open houses. These surveys were designed to help us discover the assets in the community, along with the self-perceived needs of the community. At one home, a man patiently answered our questions about the perceived needs that he saw in the community, and when we came to the part of the survey where we asked him to share the assets he saw, he said to us, "I've been living here for years, I've seen programs and organizations come in and out. But no one's ever asked me what I can do, what my talents are, what my dreams are, much less what I think the problems and solutions might be. I'm a retired building contractor and worked in the construction industry for twenty years. I've dreamed about passing on those skills to others. Could I do that?"

If all we do is assess needs, we reinforce the idea that the community is needy and dependent, unable to help itself. We communicate that the community has nothing to offer, that they get to receive, sit back, and applaud when the work gets done. Instead, however, we need to remember that each community and every person in that community has God-given resources. Those assets may be latent or forgotten, and sometimes they are hard to find. But this is the "hidden treasure" that God uses to accomplish the work of transformation. If you take a bottom-up approach:

- *You increase ownership.* People tend to have a much higher vested interest in the success of something that was their idea. People are committed because they have something of value to bring to the table as well.
- *You filter "fake" objectives.* If you develop legitimate ownership, you often learn the difference between the "real" and the "fake" objectives. If the community is not going to be asked to contribute its talent or be accountable to the outcomes, then who really cares what happens?
- *You build realistic objectives.* People like to succeed. If you have community buy-in and ownership, then people tend to be more realistic about what they're going to help to implement. If it's "all you," then there can be unrealistic demands made on your ability to execute.

Need-Based: Targets what is lacking in a community and seeks to compensate through resources from the outside. "What do you need?"	**Asset-Based:** Targets what resources already exist from within a community to identify both a starting point and what is most important for implementation. "What do you already have?"

Codependent versus Self-Sustaining and Reproducible

Our friends worked out a partnership with a larger training network. "We'll host thirty huge conferences and train more than a hundred thousand leaders this year in India." They invited two hundred churches here in the States to "own" a conference, which meant sending in a pastor to teach the standardized material at the conference. "We're going to train one hundred thousand leaders in one year!" It feels like something a local church should jump all over. Ten years later, however, we wonder, How can we measure what the impact of those conferences was? Who implemented what? What success did they have? How much, if anything, was multiplied or reproduced?

Instead of hosting a large training event, we chose a different approach. Our goal was to keep things small, organic, and highly relational. All the training was done in small gatherings of about thirty people led by people who had successfully implemented what they were teaching in a similar context. Every learner was partnered with a coach, a successful practitioner who met with the learner regularly to problem solve, track the data, and celebrate wins. As each batch of new leaders was trained, new coaches and trainers were identified and equipped. Every person in the movement was equipped to be a reproducing Christian. And every church in the movement was equipped to be a reproducing church.

Demonstration farm

We call this training process *demonstration farming.* Here where we live in Indiana we have corn. In addition to corn, we have corn, corn, and more corn. But if you drive through rural areas in other parts of the United States, you will come across farms where different sections of the field are planted with different varieties of corn or beans. These are called demonstration farms. Demonstration farming is a strategy for introducing changes in farming methods. The demonstration of different yields for different varieties of crops influences the buying decisions of farmers in that area in the next planting season. Borrowing from this idea, we've begun planting "demonstration farms" with our partners in India. We move into an area at the grassroots level, find a few early adopters, help them implement a change, and then help them reproduce the change. After doing this for several years, we've observed the following seasons of growth (fig. 6.2):

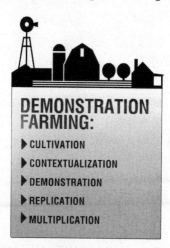

Figure 6.2

Cultivation (12 Months)

1. *Community.* We begin building relationships and identify a small number of influential indigenous people.
2. *Exposure.* We become familiar with local challenges and opportunities faced by these churches and their vision for ministry.

3. *Introduce*. We introduce the new idea/concept/resource and share the impact it has had on the church/community/world.
4. *Evaluate*. We assess the potential for partnership.

Contextualization (12–18 Months)

1. *Translation into Culture*. We present ideas, innovations, and concepts in detail to a select group of local church leaders. Local churches "add the spice," contextualizing the teaching and making it their own.
2. *Ownership*. We begin the process of transferring possession of the idea or concept to indigenous leadership.

Demonstration (12–18 Months)

1. *Selection*. Local church leaders select a group of early adopters.
2. *Training and Coaching*. Expatriates and local leaders provide in-depth training and coaching.
3. *Tracking*. Results are monitored and there is a visible demonstration of the impact.
4. *Resources*. Materials are printed for the use of the demonstration group (1.0 version). The demonstration group field-tests the materials and suggests improvements.

Replication (Ongoing)

1. *Transition*. Increased levels of leadership move to the local level with each cycle of coaching.
2. *Expansion*. We develop a separate training to train the trainers and coach the coaches.
3. *Decentralization*. We encourage churches and coaches to become champions of new works in other networks or regions.

Multiplication (Until Jesus Returns)
This is where it gets crazy. By this point, the coaching of leaders has been decentralized, and churches are being regularly challenged to

move toward the unreached people groups in their region. Even if the Western church that initially sponsored the movement disappeared, the movement itself would not stop. It has become self-sustaining and reproducing. Most of the time, you can't even keep track of what's going on because the movement is multiplying at too many layers to possibly track all that is happening.

One of our Indian coaches, a man named Anbuvanan, used to sneak out on his wife in the middle of the night. But he wasn't having an affair—he was sneaking away to be trained as a church planter! Still, like many pastors, serving the church had become Anbuvanan's top priority, and his family was getting nothing but the leftovers.

Anbuvanan and his wife

His marriage was broken. After receiving the church planter training we provided, Anbuvanan not only experienced spiritual renewal in his own life and in his church; he began to experience it in his relationship with his wife and family. Our coaching wasn't just strategy and tactics for mission; it provided development in all areas of life. Over the next eighteen months, Anbuvanan's wife saw her husband transformed into a new man, one who overflowed with love and affection for her and their children. Where she had once resented the church, now she wanted to become a part of its mission. Instead of two people living in separate worlds, the two had become one, stunning those who knew them. Several of their neighbors noticed the difference in their marriage and began inquiring about how they too could have a marriage like theirs.

Anbuvanan shared with me, "Since the coaching, our church has already planted eight more churches in this district. Also, I have begun coaching other church leaders outside our church plants. Since I began coaching them, they have planted more than ninety other churches among the untouchables. As a result, more than five thousand new believers have been baptized in this region."

That's just one coach. That's what we mean when we talk about self-sustaining, reproducible movements. They start small, but produce big results.

Codependent: Typically employ high-cost or complex initiatives that are difficult to replicate or turn over to an indigenous people. Local population is encouraged to benefit, but not to "own." "This is our ship in your waters. Welcome aboard."	**Self-Sustaining and Reproducible:** Initiatives are designed at the outset to be turned over to a target population, are defined in terms of length of time and resources, and are intended to help the target population to replicate the initiatives elsewhere. "This is your ship, and we're just helping you build it. Better learn to sail."

All of the differences we have shared illustrate the power of "smallness" in action—the value of thinking bottom-up instead of top-down. In this age of big, mass-produced, supersized solutions, we need to constantly ask ourselves, "Does it really work?" and "Will it last?" Big is not always better. In fact, it may not help you to achieve the goal you intend. Small seeds, when planted and tended, can bear much fruit. These bottom-up approaches reflect the countercultural perspective of the kingdom, and they have the potential to unleash more transformational power than is humanly possible, despite our best efforts and biggest solutions.

Chapter 7

FROM DIFFUSED TO FOCUSED
Missional Move 7

I (Rob) grew up in a big "missions" church. Our vision for God's work in the world was embodied in one key symbol: the thumbtack-filled world map. In the church foyer, we had a large world map positioned behind the coat racks, and on that map, dozens of thumbtacks were strategically stuck at various locations around the world. Dangling from each tack was a piece of yarn, stretched out and attached to a picture of a missionary or an agency card. The objective of our mission work was clear and obvious to all of us: "How many thumbtacks can we get on that board?" We all knew that the more thumbtacks you had, the more involved you were in the work of the Great Commission. There was a sense of urgency to it all, and we were constantly working to support more and more missionaries and ministries so we could get more done for the Great Commission. After all, more is better!

Our story is not that unique. We all know of countless churches that are involved with dozens of ministries and missionaries, and most of them are striving to add more every year. Maybe you are in a church like this. Believe me, I understand your passion and can relate to the commitment behind "more is better." Most of the time, churches like this have a clear passion for the Great Commission. But let's take a closer look at our motives for mission and consider this question: "Is it possible that in our pursuit of 'more' in the name of the Great Commission, we've made our mission the Great Commotion instead of God's mission?"

LASER VERSUS FLASHLIGHT

We call the "more is better" way of thinking the Flashlight Approach. Like a flashlight, light is diffused to shine on as many places as possible. A flashlight only manages to flash a thin layer of light so it can cover as much real estate as possible. It shines a photon-thick film over everything, but it doesn't really change anything in the room.

But what if we took that same light and focused it? Now you'd have a laser. I (Jack) once worked for a company whose sister organization was involved in sheet-metal fabrication. In their metal shop, they owned several laser cutters which could cut a half inch of steel as effortlessly as scissors cutting paper. In the right hands, a laser can be used to burn off cancerous growth. In the right hands, a laser can restore sight to a person who is legally blind.

The difference between the laser and the flashlight is the power of focus. This is our next missional move: a shift from being diffused to focused.

LESS IS MORE

At Granger, we've opted to model what we do after the laser instead of the flashlight. Using the Acts 1:8 framework, we have sought to narrow our focus rather than broaden it, limiting ourselves to one primary focus in each of the following areas:

Jerusalem (Local Access). For our Jerusalem, we are focused locally on Monroe Circle, a single, low-income housing neighborhood in South Bend, Indiana.

Judea (Domestic Access). For our Judea, our domestic focus, we have chosen to work in a neighborhood in Chicago known as "Little India."

Samaria (Cross-Cultural Access, All Locations). Samaria was characterized by a significant cultural divide. The Samaritans had a different culture, history, and religion from the Jews. So, the newly sent apostles would need to equip themselves for a certain "crossing over" that had less to do with their geography and more to do with culture. Because we live in the United States, we can have a cross-cultural experience at any of the other three areas: local, domestic, or international. That's why we don't pinpoint a specific Samaria geography but try to ensure that all the other points are as cross-culturally potent as possible.

Ends of the Earth (International Access). Our focus on the "ends of the earth" is limited to the area of Tamil Nadu, India, and within that area, we have made the city of Trichy the epicenter of our work.

In each sphere of influence, 80 percent of our time, energy, manpower, and resources flow into a single focused work of ministry. We've intentionally chosen to go thirty feet deep in three places rather than three inches deep in thirty places. This is the idea that "less is more" — focused work in a few areas can lead to greater effectiveness. When people first look at what Granger Community Church does, they often say, "That's *all* you do? A church your size should be ashamed of itself! One neighborhood in South Bend? One state in one nation internationally? You don't support any career missionaries? What's wrong with you? I thought you said you were committed to the Great Commission!" We find that these responses reflect a misunderstanding of the nature of focused ministry. By working in fewer places, we actually end up doing more. This limited focus gives us great liberty to invest in ideas and opportunities that will have a laserlike, permanent, and indelible impact on the places where we do choose to focus.

Excellence matters. When you are looking for quality, you limit the options. The finest restaurants typically have only a few items on the menu, whereas gigantic buffets may serve everything, but the quality of the food is suspect. We want our expression of mission to be the equivalent of a four-star, world-class meal. That doesn't mean that you can't have quantity and quality (we believe that you can!), but you have to strive for quality first. Many churches put quantity first in their mission effort and never get the quality they want.

Activity does not equal success. Activity and results are not the same thing. Like water flowing through a hose filled with holes, your mission will lack power when you are invested in too many projects and supporting too many programs and people, no matter how worthy they may be. When we spend years adding more, it ends up draining our effectiveness. Activity in the area of mission does not necessarily equal success.

Impact is more important than immediate gratification. Simply dropping teams here and there and throwing money at the latest opportunity to give is not a strategic way to advance the kingdom. While supporting new people and seeing the tacks on the board grow can feel very gratifying, we ultimately have to evaluate whether what we are doing is really the most strategic stewardship of our time and resources. In the long run, it is nearly impossible to measure the impact of the diffused approach to mission. With a more focused approach, we are able to position every short-term team, financial investment, and extension of our people and resources as part of our effort to build a long-term mission and accomplish our long-term goals. Every little investment we make adds up to a big impact over time.

FINDING FOCUS

So how does your local church move from being diffused to focused? How do you find your focus? Have you ever been to the eye doctor for an eye exam? If you have, you know that they seat you in a chair with a contraption filled with lenses that come down in front of your face. The first set of lenses snaps into place and the questioning begins. "Is this clear?" Then the lens is switched. "Is that better or is this better?" If you're a type A person like me, this entire process can be kind of stressful—you don't want to fail the test! Still, you can rest assured knowing that if you push through the trial of the eye exam, at the end of the day you will find clarity and focus.

We believe that finding your focus is a function of two things: smart thinking and Spirit-led prompting. Each of these work just like a lens clicking into place. Both lenses are necessary, and in each one we seek not to "lean on our own understanding" (Prov. 3:5–6), as if the process were merely a human and strategic effort. The goal is to use these lenses to bring clarity and focus, discovering the unique contribution that your church can make to the kingdom.

Smart Thinking

The Smart Thinking lens helps us to see that whatever a church does "outside of its walls" should be a reflection of who it is "inside its walls." Mark Beeson, the senior pastor of Granger Community Church, has always provided great clarity about why our church exists. We knew at the outset that whatever we did on mission, locally or globally, it would need to be an extension of who we are—our core DNA. As we discussed in Missional Move 5, we began working with the fluency concept, seeking to identify our "affluence." Where has God made us rich? How can we best share with the world the unique blessing God has given the people of our church? To better articulate your core identity as a local church, we recommend that you take some time to view your current church body through the following six lenses:

1. Our Heritage

   - What were the dreams/intentions of the founding pastor/pastors of our church?
   - What are some of the greatest successes in our history?
   - What were some of the contributing factors to these successes?
   - What are some of the challenges that we have faced in the past and how did we respond to them?
   - What are some of the things that we've learned over the years as a church?

2. Our Strengths

   - What do we do well as a church?
   - What are the things that we do easily?
   - What aspects of our church do we feel good about?
   - What positive things happen spontaneously in our church, without a great deal of strategic planning?
   - When our community at large talks about us, how do they describe us?

3. Our Senior Leadership

   - How is God currently speaking through our leaders?
   - In what direction is the leadership voice in our church taking us?
   - What are the greatest strengths of our senior leadership team?

4. Our Current Spiritual Season

   - What season is our church currently experiencing?
   - What are the indicators of this season?
   - About what specific things is God speaking to us as a church in this season?
   - How does this season influence our mission?

5. Our Resources

- What types of resources has God placed abundantly within our church?
- Is there interconnectedness between our resources? (Do they represent a common theme?)
- What type of people has God attracted to our church?
- Can we identify a unique people resource within our church?
- Can we identify a mission need that these resources could meet?

6. God's Revelation

- What is God currently saying to us as a church about our mission?
- Are there recurring future statements spoken about our church from within the congregation or from visitors? What theme do they carry?
- When people in the congregation speak about the future of the church, what "sense" do they have about it? What do they "feel" God is going to do through the church?

We have summarized our answers to these questions, viewed through these six lenses, in our mission, vision, and values statements. In our early days, we spent our time figuring out what all of this looked like in the way it was expressed "inside the box"—in our weekend services, our church ministries, volunteers, classes, and so on. Then, ten years ago, we began to aggressively ask, "What does it look like to express our uniqueness *outside* of the box on mission, both locally and globally?"

Eventually, we came up with a new way of seeing everything—our life mission values statement (see *missionalmoves.com*). At that time, this was our "best guess" as to what the DNA of the church would look like out in the world. The life mission values statement was helpful because it provided us with a filter to consider the endless opportunities in front of us. We set up missional experiments in several different environments, both locally and internationally, using our wisdom and making the best decisions we could. But that's as far as we could go with this lens. Then we needed those Spirit-led promptings.

Spirit-Led Prompting

At the same time that we are exercising wisdom and evaluating opportunities that match our unique calling as a body, we must listen and look for the leadership of the Holy Spirit. Where is God at work? How can we join him? As we live on mission, we keep our eyes open for the opportunities that "pop" out of the landscape of opportunities in front of us. At Granger, as we combined smart thinking with Spirit-led promptings, things slowly came into focus for us.

Locally, this led to our focus on the Monroe Circle neighborhood. The point of origin for this work actually began in Chicago. One of our short-term "experiment" teams was serving in a low-income housing project in that city. Over the course of the trip, the team fell in love with the kids they served. When it came time to leave, the kids came up with hope in their eyes asking our team members, "When are you going to be back?" That question devastated some of the team members because all they could say was, "I don't know ... maybe next summer." The kids' faces dropped. If you are a child trapped in poverty in an urban ghetto, "next summer" is the same as saying, "Never!"

Two women on that team, Jodi and Sandra, were especially affected by their interactions with the children. On the bus ride home to Indiana, these two women sensed a holy discontent stirring within them. They began talking with their team leader, saying, "We don't have to go to Chicago to do this; we have projects in our own hometown. We ought to do this at home. That way we could serve the kids on a regular basis." The team leader, Dan Blacketor,

EnterMission Story // Diffused to Focus
Dustin Holiday, Director of Outreach
Christian Fellowship Church, Ashburn, Virginia

When I joined the missions committee of my church, I learned that we were supporting more than fifty missionaries and indigenous ministry workers in more than twenty countries. It felt like we were doing so many good things all over the world. All that we had to do was send the checks, pray a little, hold a conference once a year, send occasional teams, and by doing all these things, we could say that our church did "missions" and a lot of it. Over the next few years, we picked up even more as our budget grew, and in 2006, we were supporting seventy-four missionaries in more than twenty-five countries! It definitely made for an exciting pin map in our hallway.

In early 2007, however, God called me to leave my decade-long career as a police officer and take on the role of outreach director for the church. Immediately, I realized that no one actually knew very much about what those seventy-four people did. So I hit the road. In the following eighteen months, I spent twenty weeks traveling and visiting these folks. I learned firsthand about some amazing things God was doing in the world. Unfortunately, I also saw some really unamazing things. As I returned from those experiences, I found myself experiencing a holy discontent about the lack of a clear vision for what Christian Fellowship Center was trying to accomplish with our global mission expression. There was no focus and little engagement. In most cases, there was no deep connection between the DNA of CFC and the work we supported.

In 2009, I joined the EnterMission Coaching Network and began an eighteen-month journey to discover how to really take CFC on mission in the world. This missional move spoke to my discontent. We knew we had to go from diffused to focused. Using several diagnostic tools created by EnterMission, I was able to take the leadership of CFC through the process of identifying our missional DNA. Through lots of conversation and prayer, we found where and how God was calling us to focus. Today, in 2011, our main focus is our church-to-church partnership with the Verbo church in Puerto Cabezas, Nicaragua. We also have smaller partnerships in Haiti and Ghana. We have gone from supporting seventy-four missionaries to twenty-one. Lest that cause a heart attack when you read it, we were able to make the transition with grace and dignity, without bloodshed, without people leaving our church, and, seemingly unbelievably, with most of our missionaries actually being encouraged by our willingness to participate in God's mission, even if that no longer included them financially.

I have been in awe at how progressing from diffused to focused within our global expression has changed the face of our congregation. Before, no one knew what we did globally, and scarcely a person could name a missionary we support. Before, we would have a smattering of people participate in short-term global trips. But today almost everyone knows where we go and why, and we are sending more than two hundred people annually to our focus areas. The experiences our members have had by being a part of a focused mission globally has spilled over now into our local mission expression. Before we didn't even really have a local mission, but today we have more than fifteen hundred people mobilized on mission here at home serving our city.

Equally important, if not more important, is the change in impact we have seen in our focus area. Within our main partnership in Nicaragua, we went from just sending checks and supporting random projects to having a long-term shared vision for holistic ministry in specific communities. Today we can go to communities that look and feel different after less than two years of "focusing." We are dedicated to staying fiercely focused after having seen just a sample of what going from diffused to focused will produce for God's kingdom!

acknowledged the truth of what they were suggesting, and told them, "You are right. You ought to think about that. In fact, you ought to do something about it." They asked Dan where they should get started, and Dan wisely encouraged them to begin with some assessment: "Why don't you start with the South Bend Housing Authority. Learn from those who live in and serve the community. Ask them what is already happening and how you could fit in."

When these two women, full of great intentions, first approached our local Housing Authority asking if there was any way that they could help, they were solidly rejected and informed that they were not welcome. When the women asked why, the Housing Authority director said, "I can't tell you how many churches come in over the years and say, 'We want to help the kids.' They show up and do their program for a couple of hours, their games, crafts, snacks, and the whole routine. Then it always builds to the same thing. They lead the kids in the sinner's prayer, count the noses, do a little dance, and then they are gone. They go home thinking about what amazing Christians they are for going and helping the poor people, and then we never see them again."

Then the Housing Authority director leaned across her desk said something that has echoed through our department and our church for more than a decade since: "The people in this community have enough issues with abandonment without the church adding to it."

In response, Jodi and Sandra humbly shared their heartbreaking experience in Chicago, how they wanted to do more than a quick program. They shared their desire for something more consistent, something that would last. The director hesitated, but eventually agreed, saying, "We'll try it. I'm giving you a little box. No preaching. No proselytizing. You can teach the kids values and life skills, but if you color outside the lines, I'll shut you down and you'll never work in another Housing Authority environment again. Got it?"

Delighted that they had been granted an opportunity, the women asked the director where the greatest opportunity was to invest in the community. In response, the director laughed. "You're standing in it. The Monroe Circle community is the lowest income, most abandoned, most forgotten community in the Authority. And if you're here, I can keep an eye on you. You can start here."

With the beachhead established by these two ladies and with a laser focus in this small community, God began to pour out his favor. Jodi and Sandra began a mentoring program called Son City Kids, which quickly exploded in size. What began with Jodi, Sandra, and seven kids at a picnic table soon ballooned into more than one hundred volunteers serving hundreds of kids. God was clearly smiling on our efforts, and the staff at Granger stood by in awe at what God was doing. We were learning a simple truth as well: if you love kids well, you make their parents happy. That love creates goodwill in a neighborhood. And when scores of parents find something to celebrate, seeing the blessing of God poured out upon their kids, that word gets back to the South Bend Housing Authority.

A few years after starting the Son City Kids mentoring program, we were in a meeting with several of the movers and shakers among the nonprofits in our community. The meeting was intended to help facilitate greater collaboration between the various nonprofit organizations on behalf of the poor. The host of the meeting began introducing the people present. We were at the meeting representing Granger. After we were introduced to the group, the director of the Housing Authority, the same person who had given Jodi and Sandra a chilly greeting, raised her hand. "I don't want to interrupt," she said, "but I just have to say something." She stood to her feet and proclaimed, "I'm glad Granger Community Church is represented today. I just want to say that Granger Community Church is my favorite church in this whole community, and I don't even go there. They are the real deal. Whatever they want to do in any of the areas overseen by the South Bend Housing Authority is fine with me!"

We were shocked. Things had certainly changed from that first meeting with Sandra and Jodi! God was now blessing us with favor in our community.

Shortly afterward, several other pieces of the puzzle fell into place. Unexpectedly, another team developed from within our congregation with a shared concern for the single moms in the Monroe Circle community. They began offering a home and life management course called Life Basics. Then, much to our surprise, we discovered that there was a food pantry operating a few times a month in a run-down, empty building across the street. It mainly served the elderly people of the neighborhood and was stocked and run by a few elderly men and women who purchased food out of their own pocketbooks for those who most needed it. Over a period of time, after building some relationships with the people operating the pantry, the men and women running it asked our church if we would take over the pantry's operation in exchange for the building in which it operated.

The condemnable conditions of the building where the food pantry was housed began to prick the hearts of several others at our church. This group began rallying others in the church to find tables and set up a café environment, even forging a partnership with Panera Bread to provide fresh pastries and coffee to go along with the food distribution. They painted the walls and added new lights and sparkle to the building. They also equipped a first-impressions team of greeters: folks who were there to serve coffee, talk with people, and pray for their needs. Suddenly, we realized that a genuine community was forming. The barriers of poverty and fear, which tend to isolate people from one another, were giving way to conversations and relationships. These were people who had lived near each other for years, but had never talked. New friendships were forming. We knew God was up to something.

The leading of the Spirit was bringing clear focus to our calling. Beginning with Son City Kids, the mentoring ministry for single moms, then the food pantry, and then, suddenly, the gift of a building in Monroe Circle—we knew that God was telling us something. At this point, the organized church of Granger began to formally support the micromovement of the people of God, and we became aware that our presence as the people of God in the Monroe Circle community was indeed a Spirit-led prompting. Together we realized Jesus wanted an outpost for the kingdom in this neighborhood, and he was calling us as a local church to be present there.

Since that time, the little food pantry has become a fully functional community center spanning an entire city block. Through a number of partnerships with local government agencies, schools, and businesses, we now offer GED courses, family literacy classes, financial teaching, vocational training, help with job placement, several athletic programs, and, of course, the mentoring and food pantry programs. There is also a weekly community that gathers for worship, Bible study, and leadership development called The Gathering.

Narrowing our focus to Monroe Circle has dramatically increased our impact. Without that focus, these smaller interventions would stand alone, separated from each other and scattered wide across the community. But with that laser focus, everything we do is connected, building a clear sense of collaboration as one team hands the baton of mission to the next.

Consider the following two diagrams. Which of them illustrates the impact you want for your church?

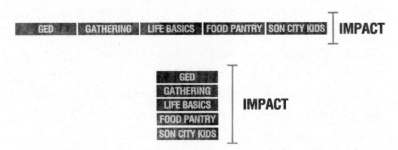

The missional move we are highlighting here—from diffused to focused—has the power to release God's power into lives and communities in ways that lead to lasting, measurable change. Imagine a movement of churches with this kind of focus, who have identified neighborhoods and villages all over the world where they are radically committed for the long haul. In these laser-focused locations, they begin to pour out their lives and resources to help advance the kingdom of God.

Chapter 8

FROM TRANSACTIONAL TO TRANSFORMATIONAL PARTNERSHIPS

Missional Move 8

During our first fifteen years at Granger, we focused our energy on reaching our Jerusalem: our unreached friends, family, neighbors, and coworkers. And we have no regrets about that. We firmly believe the light that shines the farthest is the light that shines the brightest at home. If you skip reaching your Jerusalem on your way to reach the ends of the earth, something is out of order.

During that season, however, our local and global expressions of mission were disjointed. Our mission efforts—in Judea and in Samaria and to the ends of the earth—didn't reflect our calling and identity as a church, our DNA. Everything we did was done in "support mode." The men of the church supported an international housing organization and made periodic trips to build houses. The women supported a shelter for unwed mothers. The youth had their own projects. These were all good things. And this is what many churches do. Find a good organization and support them. The problem with support mode is that it doesn't lead to long-term growth. It's an approach that offers a form of life support, sustaining a patient's life while they remain critically ill or injured. Picture someone lying in a hospital bed with feeding tubes, IV lines, and a respirator. Remaining in support mode is not really a good place to be, is it? It's the spiritual equivalent of providing feeding tubes to chosen organizations, giving them a slow trickle of volunteers and money to keep things running.

In the midst of our growth in Jerusalem, we heard the Spirit's voice inviting us to open our hearts even wider. We sensed that the time had come for us to bring the same kind of intentionality and ownership to our expression of mission in our Judea, Samaria, and to the ends of the earth. We were determined to get off the life-support approach to our mission as a local church. We were convinced that God's plan was for us to be fully alive in every area of influence he was providing for us: locally, regionally, domestically, and internationally. As we set out, we found that yet another missional move was needed. We quickly found that our support-mode approach to mission was rooted in an entrenched partnership model that was effectively strangling our freedom to grow and respond as a local church. We realized that the time had come for us to make yet another shift, from *transactional* partnerships to *transformative* ones.

TRANSACTIONAL PARTNERSHIPS

Here's what we discovered very quickly: the work of mission "out there" is largely owned and operated by organizations. While there are a small but growing number of pioneering organizations exploring more collaborative ways to partner with the local church, most organizations still want to make a transaction with the church, one built primarily around financial support. The local church is seen as a big wallet, and the goal of the relationship is to open that wallet to fund the organization's mission. The process of a local church developing a partnership usually looks something like this (fig. 8.1):

Figure 8.1

Step 1: The church forms a missions board. Usually, this is a group of passionate volunteers or possibly staff. The primary function of the team is the distribution of funding to organizations and missionaries. This typically includes the organization of volunteer opportunities and short-term trips.

Step 2: The missions board selects an organization. The local church looks for an organization to hire. Personal passions and previous relationships drive the focus, not the DNA of the local church.

Step 3: The church hires the organization. The local church hires a partner organization (or several organizations) to carry out the work of mission, outsourcing the work of mission to the organization. The local church adopts and supports the mission of the agency or organization.

In the transactional model of partnership, an agency owns and operates the work of mission. The agency works directly with the indigenous people, whether that is the homeless population in your town or an unreached people group on the other side of the planet. If it's a good organization, it effectively accomplishes the mission vision. The churches are planted. The wells are dug. The homeless are sheltered. The hungry are fed. The illiterate learn to read.

Often, great work is being done by these organizations. That's not the problem. The problem is the way the local church relates to the mission. Where does the local church stand in this partnership? The people themselves sit safely in the comfort of the sanctuary, outside of the mission flow. Periodically, a few select individuals will cross the divide as volunteers or as part of a short-term team, tagging along with the organization. But it is the organization, not the church, that actually owns the mission. The organization works hard to give the church a sense of ownership, but the plain truth is that local churches aren't involved in the direct flow of mission. At worst, transactional partnerships leave us with churchless organizations and missionless churches.

Ironically, many times both the local church and the hired partners are quite happy with this asset-based relationship. The hired organization gets the funding they need to carry out the mission vision. The sponsoring local church gets to take credit for the work that is done without having to do any of the actual work of mission. But we are convinced that this divorce between the local church and the work of mission is not God's plan A. It's a poor substitute for the true mission of the church. The local church is God's plan A, and this means we need a new model of partnership.

TRANSFORMATIONAL PARTNERSHIPS

In *transformational* partnerships we move beyond a money-driven, organization-centered, one-dimensional way of relating toward mission. Instead, we move to a kingdom-centered, multidimensional

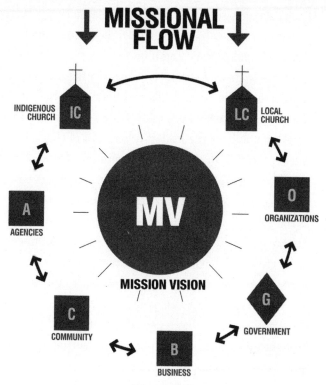

Figure 8.2

way of relating to mission (fig. 8.2). In this new model of partnership, the local church becomes the catalyst for a web of relationships, all built around a shared mission vision for a specific context. The vision for community transformation is expansive, involving people from different domains of society. The local church begins by relating to different parties among the indigenous people: people in nonprofit organizations, government agencies, businesses, other churches, even leaders of other faiths. These parties begin exploring how to work together toward a common goal. This model depends upon several key factors:

1. *A shared mission vision.* A mission vision statement is developed together with other partners. This mission vision represents more than just the goals of a single organization.

Each party has elements that drive the agenda, and it is comprised of a shared focus, shared work, shared values, shared resources, and genuine community.

2. *Everyone leads and everyone follows.* In the older model of partnership, one party leads and everyone else parties. In the new model, everybody takes leadership in some way, and everybody follows the lead of others. All of this is based on the expertise, affluence, and contribution that each partner possesses. In addition, everyone defers to others who may have expertise in other areas and insists on true confluence as the goal.

3. *Everyone gives and everyone receives.* In the old model, one party gives and the others receive. In the new model, as each party turns their affluence into influence, the confluence leads to effluence. At that point, everyone has given something and everyone has received something. We have each brought our wealth to the mission, offsetting each other's poverty. In so doing, we are all enriched.

Transformational partnership is love in action. We come together out of our separate lives, industries, sectors, and constraining frameworks to accomplish a shared mission, one birthed by the love of God. In the process, we are all transformed.

So how, exactly, do the players from all these different sectors of society work together?

THE CAR MODEL

All sectors of society must be engaged to experience holistic transformation in a given community. Unfortunately, collaboration between different sectors is often nonexistent or ineffective because each of the sectors lacks a clear understanding of their role in the larger framework. We illustrate these interactions between the various sectors using the metaphor of a car.

Moving Graphics, www.movinggraphics.com

While the car model isn't perfect, and we recognize its limitations, we offer it as a starting point—an on-ramp—for discussions about collaboration and partnership. In order for a car to run safely on the road and arrive at its intended destination, it requires some critical elements: wheels and chassis, engine and drive train, as well as additional components (things like a steering wheel, seats, and airbags). In addition to these three elements, you will also need a well-paved, safely governed roadway to travel on.

The Wheels and Chassis. Faith communities are the ultimate grassroots organizations. They are deeply embedded in cultures and societies all over the globe. In many cases, the leaders of these faith communities have a vested interest in the health and transformation of their communities. They are like the wheels and chassis of a car. They are closest to the ground. Without them, you really aren't getting anywhere. But without the help of others in the community, they are little more than "Flintstone" mobiles. You have to run fast, push hard, and then hop on board—but you only travel for twenty feet. It's not the ideal way to get where you want to go. Other "parts" are required.

The Engines. Businesses tend to focus on efficiency. They are committed to the bottom line: economic profitability and sustainability. They are the "engines" of the car, providing the drive, focus, efficiency, and financial resources needed to power a collaborative venture. Yet their transformative power is limited to the ways in which they are connected to the chassis of the faith community. A socially conscious business will not simply seek a bottom-line profit for its owners; it will seek the good of the community in which it operates. Without a connection to a faith community, the engine is running "on blocks." It may crank out profit for the personal benefit of a few, but it's not really going anywhere for the community.

The Components of the Car. For the last two hundred years, external organizations have led the efforts in mission and community transformation. As a result, they have become exceedingly efficient in targeting problems and working out solutions. Their dedication to a particular area of focus makes them ideal "components" to the car, but they are not the car itself. A steering wheel manufacturer, for instance, does not go to Ford and say, "Your job is to make a car that will adequately support and showcase our steering wheel!" Rather, the job of the steering wheel manufacturer is to provide a component that helps the car get where it needs to go. Nongovernmental organizations (NGOs) and mission or aid organizations have a similar function. The car is not there to support their work. Rather, they serve a unique role, as part of the vehicle, enabling the car to get where it needs to go.

The Road. What is the role of the government in all of this? We do not believe it's the responsibility of government, at any level, to implement transformation. It can't. It's not close enough to the people, and governments simply cannot facilitate the kinds of relationships necessary to provide for that kind of change. What governments can provide are the conditions that lead to an environment conducive to transformation. Governments have immense system-building and infrastructure capacity. They can provide leadership, legislation, and enforcement of the law. In short, governments can provide the environment that enables transformation to occur, much like the roads and signs needed for safe travel. Roads (governments) make transformational movement easier, marking the way forward so that people know where they're going and how to get there.

The purpose of the car model is to illustrate how and where everyone's expertise is most valuable in the process of community transformation. Usually we have little difficulty defining who is running which component on the ground. Still, you may wonder, "What does this really look like in practice?" Let's consider an example of what it looks like to drive the car of community transformation in India.

Twenty-nine long hours by plane and three hours by jeep will bring you to an unassuming colony of untouchables living outside the city of Kalavai in Tamil Nadu, India. The people of this colony are of the Irula caste.

Meet Kasi at *missionalmoves.com*. Look for the video called "Kasi."

They are at the bottom rung of the ladder in India. A man named Kasi is the head village elder, and he has watched generational poverty grind his people into the dust.

A few years ago, many of the people in the Irula caste in Kalavai were homeless, living under trees or in huts made out of thatch and garbage. Most lived on one meal. They had no electricity or clean water. Disease was rampant. There were no educational opportunities available for their children. Men were trapped on the lowest rung of the vocational ladder, working as rat and snake catchers. They were truly a people living without hope.

Today, however, every family in the colony has good housing. The huts they used to live in have been demoted to storage sheds. A new well flows in the village, providing clean water. Electricity runs to every home. The children of the village attend school. Micro-enterprises have broken the chains of poverty and inspire a creative, entrepreneurial spirit. A new community center has been built.

The village elder, Kasi, describes the transformation as a flower that has sprouted, grown, and blossomed. Where the spirit of the people was dying, choked by the dust and weeds of poverty and oppression, now there is life and beauty: "For centuries, it had been told to us that the Brahman people have sprung from the heads of the gods and the Irula people came from the dust on the bottom of the gods' feet. Our name, Irula, means 'People of Darkness.' Since Pastor Sam and the people of Granger have come, no longer do we know ourselves as the people of darkness. We know ourselves now as the people of light!" Soon after the changes began transforming life in the village, the water from the new well washed over Kasi himself. He was baptized as a follower of Jesus Christ.

Behind this radical story of transformation is a surprising list of partners, a group of incredibly diverse people who united around a mission vision. Over the past five years, that team has included hundreds of people from Granger Community Church, virtually every single community member of the village, many of the people from the indigenous local church, as well as people in the local government, local contractors, local businesses, and some wonderful individuals from international organizations like World Relief and Hydraid. All of these people were attracted to a kingdom vision — the transformation of a little colony of untouchables.

At this point, you might be thinking: "This all sounds great, but let's get practical. How do you actually build the car? What is the process?" We began by recognizing that the work in India was already underway long before we got there. And this will always be true. Jesus said, "My Father and I are always at work." The transformational partnership process doesn't begin with the question, "What can we do?" It begins with the question, "What is God already doing?"

THE PROCESS

The process of transformational partnership has three phases: mission building, capacity building, and direct ministry. We learned this descriptive language for strategic partnerships from one of our mentors, Don Golden. Don served on staff with World Relief before joining the staff of Mars Hill in Grand Rapids, Michigan. He has since returned to work on staff at World Relief as their vice president of church engagement. Don is a no-nonsense kind of guy who understands that local churches want to reclaim their God-given place in advancing the kingdom of God.

At first, the various phases happen sequentially. But then, as the partnership blossoms and grows, the three phases become a repeating cycle of evaluation that fosters deeper levels of transformation. We'll walk through each of the phases using our earlier example of our work in India.

Phase 1: Mission Building

In this first phase, a local church should ask the following four questions (fig. 8.3):

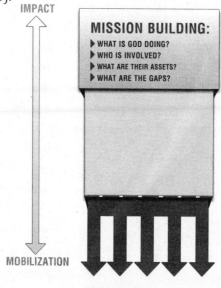

IMPACT

MISSION BUILDING:
▶ WHAT IS GOD DOING?
▶ WHO IS INVOLVED?
▶ WHAT ARE THEIR ASSETS?
▶ WHAT ARE THE GAPS?

MOBILIZATION

Figure 8.3

1. What is God doing? The first question most American local churches ask is, "What can we do?" That's a direct ministry question. It's not a bad question. As pastors and church leaders, we understand the context and essential nature of that question. However, it's a very dangerous question to start with. Why? Because before we act, we need to look and listen, watching for the ways in which God is already at work. Our invitation is to join God in his mission, not to do our own thing and then invite him to bless it. When we jump directly into ministry, we are typically focused on what we can accomplish with our resources and wisdom. Inadvertently, we can damage the development of the local people. It's often easier to do it for them, rather than doing it with them. Or even worse, we do for them what they could have done for themselves.

With that in mind, our first year of partnership development in India focused on relationship building and inquiry into the activity of God in Tamil Nadu. A church member, Ron Vandegriend, was serving as field director for Bible League International, a Bible distribution and church-planting organization. Through Ron, we learned of a church-planting movement that was spreading like wildfire. Our friends at Bible League were willing to introduce us to their network of indigenous leaders, and we went as pilgrims to learn what God was doing through our brothers and sisters in Tamil Nadu.

2. Who is involved? Three parties were involved at the start of our partnership: the people of Granger, Bible League, and a group of fifteen indigenous leaders. Among this group of leaders, our hearts were especially drawn to a man named Rajen-

RAJENDRAN: FROM TREE CLIMBER TO APOSTOLIC LEADER

If you're ready to have your faith stretched, visit *mission almoves.com* and click on the video "Rajendran" to hear Raj's full testimony. Raj's story is a modern-day example of the demoniac from Mark 8. Jesus freed him from demonic possession to lead a movement. Raj is now Granger's international director of Life Mission, overseeing all our work in India.

dran, who has since become a staff member of our Granger team. Raj, who started in a low caste as a tree climber, had by God's grace become an apostolic leader of a growing movement of church plants. As Raj and the other leaders shared with us stories of what God was doing, it felt like something ripped straight from the book of Acts.

We placed the emphasis on relating with the indigenous people before our relationships with the organizational folk back in the States. These indigenous network leaders were passionate about reproducing churches and training church planters. We asked them to orient us to their culture, their history, and their traditions. We didn't press our agenda. When they perceived that we could be trusted, they took us to the field to stay with church planters and see firsthand what was happening. They said, "We have not met foreigners like this before. We have seen many American church leaders who come to meet the 'famous' people in the big cities. But few have come to be with the faithful people who labor in obscurity on the front lines." With trust established, the foundation was laid for the next stage.

3. What are their assets? Bible League, as an organization, has several assets, including a curriculum for church-planter training, which the local people had already contextualized. Although Bible League's work in India was just beginning, their approach had proven successful in many other places, leading to more than twenty-five thousand new church plants in more than fifty nations. Our friends at Bible League also provided Granger with several opportunities to build reliable relationships with indigenous church leaders as well as the infrastructure for travel to and from various locations.

As we've stressed before, even though the indigenous church planters we met were financially poor, they were rich in many ways. Three assets stood out to us. First of all, they were rich in faith and passion for Christ. They were red-hot! Back in my college days, I (Rob) used to work in a machine shop. In the back room, they poured hot steel. When you walked into that area, the temperature would jump thirty degrees instantly, and your body would break into a sweat. Walking into the presence of these men and women of God was like walking into that back room. Your spiritual temperature would jump thirty degrees in their presence. Mission was the focus of their lives, and almost every church planter was bivocationally growing a church among the pocket of people they lived among while working a full-time job.

We also saw an asset when we looked at the rich level of community they enjoyed. Our experience in America was more typically one of isolation, living cocooned and separated from our neighbors. But in India, every village we visited functioned like a large extended family.

Finally, we saw an asset in the training and preparation provided by the network leaders. They had done an outstanding job providing basic church-planting start-up skills, contextualized for these pastors.

4. *What are the gaps?* We began to have conversations with the indigenous leaders to discern how we could add value to the assets they already possessed. What strengths did we have that we could add to their strengths and the strengths of Bible League International? What could we do that would fill in the gaps?

As we shared the story of Granger Community Church, a few things surprised them. First of all, they had never heard of a church maintaining steady growth for almost twenty years. Second, the number of people who were meaningfully engaged in service, small groups, and membership impressed them. We began to share with them our approach to church health and growth, which we had learned and adapted from the Purpose Driven Church model. They were hungry to learn more about this process of building systems within the local church to balance the purposes of the church. The average church plant within their movement would typically stall out at thirty to fifty people. The church planters had been trained in a sequential approach of church planting, and most of them didn't know how to pastor a healthy church after the start-up phase. By their own admission, many of the churches they had planted were not thriving. We had found the gap.

Phase 2: Capacity Building

In this phase, your focus is on just one question: What can we teach them to do that will multiply impact? The goal here is to build capacity in the indigenous people. We'll take a much deeper look at the "how" of capacity building in the next missional move. For now, let's return to the demonstration-farming model we introduced in chapter 6. Through an intentional process of cultivation, contextualization, demonstration, replication, and multiplication, we developed an eighteen-month coaching process for church health that has dramatically increased the health and longevity of these new church plants (fig. 8.4). At the end of the first round of coaching, almost every church we were working with had doubled or even tripled in size. The church leaders began to see improvement in the health of their faith communities, including increased numbers of people getting baptized, serving, and giving. As other church planters watched these demonstration farms thrive, they started asking, "Can I get that seed?"

As Granger added this second layer of training to existing training offered by Bible League, there was never a need for our

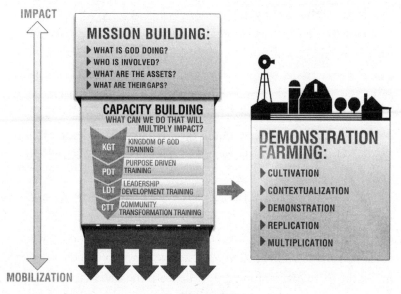

Figure 8.4

organizational partner to solicit funds from Granger to support this work. At this point, we weren't just a wallet providing money for another Bible League project, we were a strategic partner adding value to an existing work. The new training we provided went beyond the scope of the Bible League program, so Granger led and funded the work directly. Eventually, we added another two layers of training, one focused on leadership development and the other on community transformation.

Over the years, our brothers and sisters in India, most especially Raj and Ron, returned the favor to us, becoming our mentors and sharing their assets with us. We gained key insights in the work of multiplication and church planting from them. As we shared with them the church growth strategies God had used in our cultural context, they taught us from their experience in disciple making, multiplication, and reproduction. Thanks to their coaching, our church was prepared to begin several church planting initiatives following a small, organic church model.

Five years ago, working alongside Raj, we helped redesign the first level of church-planter training that had been offered by Bible League so there would be better alignment and integration between the advanced layers of coaching we had developed later. Since these changes were made, we have witnessed more than 134,000 people gathering in over a thousand churches as a part of that movement. Almost a hundred thousand people have made a confession of faith, not at big evangelistic rallies, but in the setting of small discipleship groups. More than forty thousand people have been baptized. To God be the glory!

We now call the four different capacity-building coaching tracks we developed the "bore-well" church planting model. Bore wells are common all over India. These are wells that are drilled and excavated by rotary-drilling machines. They go down hundreds of feet under the earth, penetrating deeper beneath the water table than a hand-dug well could ever go. A bore well reaches clean water that

Partnership Perspective // A Complete Recipe
Ron VanderGriend, Vice President of Development and Operations for Mission India
Former Field Director for Bible League International

From the outset of the partnership between Granger and Bible League, we always described Granger's involvement as a "value added" approach to what we were already doing on the field. This involved Bible League doing what it did best and Granger adding what Granger did best. It was a partnership between a parachurch ministry and a US-based local church that specifically allowed each agency to bring to the table something the other partner lacked. For its part, Bible League brought an on-field national staff, the ability to identify and mobilize national (Indian) partners, and a program for training church planters that was already underway. Granger added a second layer of training for select graduates of that church-planting curriculum using church-health-type materials to foster church growth for those graduates who were already experiencing success in the field. Eventually, Granger also added leadership training and community development elements to enhance those two core levels of training.

Overall, the story of Granger and Bible League is one of successful cooperation between a parachurch organization and a local church. Without Bible League, Granger's work on the ground would not have gained the necessary traction to have succeeded. Without Granger, the church planters would not have been trained to grow beyond the traditional ceilings. Both Granger and Bible League were key to a successful mission.

can provide for a village for many years. If there's water in a community, there's life. That's the purpose of a bore well.

The concept of bore-well church planting is simple. First, you plant a church in an otherwise unreached village. Then, you equip and empower that church to become the hub for community development, bringing God's living water to every area of life. This training includes (fig. 8.5):

Figure 8.5

Kingdom of God Training (KGT). Fifteen months of coaching designed to help regular people plant churches in unreached villages.

Purpose Driven Training (PDT). Fifteen months of coaching designed to build a healthy church on the five purposes: worship, evangelism, discipleship, ministry, and fellowship.

Leadership Development Training (LDT). Network leaders, trainers, and coaches are equipped to lead the movement.

Community Transformation Training (CTT). Local churches are equipped to become the hub for community development in their villages.

At each and every level of training, we seek to be:

Small and reproducing. We use a coaching model versus a conference model. We do all the training in small batches of thirty with in-field coaching. Every new batch produces new coaches and trainers.

Collaborative. From day one, we work together—the people from Granger alongside our friends in India—to develop and contextualize all the training. We continue to work together as peers on every initiative.

Reproducing. With each layer of advanced coaching, Granger carried the weight of the training in the beginning, developing more indigenous ownership and leadership in each step. Now, the first two levels of the bore well are completely run indigenously, with us halfway through transition on the last couple of levels.

BORE-WELL MODEL

If you want a deeper look into the bore-well model, you can learn more in the book *Share the Well* (*www.share-the-well-book.com*), which is also a feature-length documentary. Both the book and DVD provide an eyes-wide-open, whirlwind tour of the movement in India.

Holistic. We fused best practices in church planting with best practices in community development. This is exceedingly rare. People from Indiana and India work together building homes, teaching children, providing health care, sharing the beauty of their art, and so much more, giving hope, dignity, and skills to those without them.

At this point, it's time to answer the final question, "How do the people of Granger actually get involved?" This leads us to the final phase of transformational partnership.

Phase 3: Direct Ministry

In this phase of ministry, we ask the question, "What can our people do that will support the local people in developing their innate capabilities?"

We've sent hundreds of our people to India. We train our teams to build capacity in the members of the Indian

Want to see our people in action? Head to *missionalmoves.com* and see what direct ministry looks like for yourself.

churches and the members of the community the churches are in. We don't just do it for them. We focus on equipping them so they can do it themselves. We have teams that focus on construction, health/wellness, clean water, family life, microenterprise development, education, and the arts (fig. 8.6). All of these initiatives and teams are led by laypeople, not church staff.

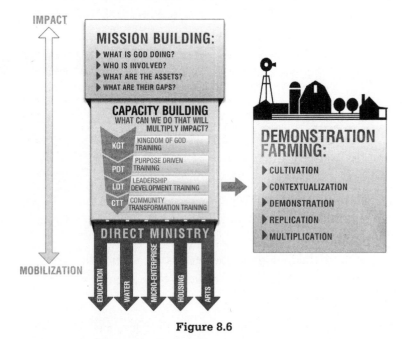

Figure 8.6

We'll unpack in more detail the process of mobilization and leadership development in two of our later missional moves. For now, here's a quick summary of how we engage in direct ministry. In the next chapter, we'll share a process we've developed to help implement all of this:

1. *We never pay the pastors or write checks to the churches directly.* We seek to enhance their work through resources like training whenever possible. Before we get involved, we want to see a local community and church assess what they can do for themselves. Once they demonstrate initiative to do this,

then we can talk about adding further projects that require outside resources. When we fund a project, we always ask the community to bring whatever resources it can, even if it's a small amount.

2. *We focus on smaller, modular training with ongoing coaching rather than large-scale, one-time conferences and events.* Ongoing coaching helps move the knowledge we share beyond just awareness of principles down to the how-to of implementation. Focusing on small projects emphasizes relationship building. These relationships give us credibility and build trust, allowing us to be involved when real, lasting changes take place.

3. *We should not habitually do something for people that they can do themselves.* Many well-meaning churches routinely violate this principle, doing serious harm to the development of the very people they are trying to help. Did we approach our ministry with local people in a truly collaborative way? Did we do it *with* them? Or did we take the easy way out and do it *for* them?

4. *We see every direct ministry project as a part of a larger process that addresses the foundational problems.* Capacity building is a slow, ongoing process of change. Underneath the symptomatic problems in any community are deep-seated foundational problems that are not quickly or easily fixed. The downward spiral that began at the tree in the Garden has created brokenness on a personal and structural level that has accumulated over the centuries. Reversing these patterns and renewing communities takes time.

5. *Every direct ministry project is seen as a "product" in a larger development process for the entire community.* A well for clean drinking water, a new church plant, a new house, a new small business, or improved crops are all products of our projects. They are easy to document and photograph. The process

used to create these products is just as important, if not more important, than the outcome. Did local people participate in the process in a way that increased their comprehension, abilities, and power?

As we close this chapter, we pray that God will give you the courage to pursue a new way of forming partnerships and that he will give you the perseverance to stay the course. William Gibson once said, "The future is already here—it's just not equally distributed." In transformational partnerships, we are pioneering a way of doing mission. Yet we're convinced that within a generation, this can become the new normal for churches in the West. As with any new endeavor, it will require pioneers who bring that future into the present with their lives.

MORE ON TRANSFORMATIONAL PARTNERSHIPS

There is more we'd love to share about this. At *missionalmoves.com* you can find two ebooks related to these topics:

Transformational Partnerships: Church to Church

Transformational Partnerships: Church to Organization

These helpful ebooks include best practices, partnership checklists, and much, much more.

The old model sent out organizations to do the work of mission, leaving the local church behind to provide money. The local church was involved, but not directly. Today, local churches are reclaiming their apostolic character. They are partnering in ways that lead to transformation. They are setting sail for uncharted waters with only the stars to guide them. Some of the tools the sailors (partner organizations) have been using remain helpful and we certainly need them. But churches themselves are sensing God's call to leave the safety of the harbor and travel the seas.

Anchors away. Let's ride the reverse tsunami together!

Chapter 9

FROM RELIEF TO DEVELOPMENT
Missional Move 9

In 1818, Mary Shelley wrote the gothic classic *Frankenstein*, the tragic tale of Victor Frankenstein, a misguided genius driven to the point of madness by his desire to create life. Scouring charnel houses and funeral homes, he pieces together raw materials, bringing them to life in a creation that he instantly despises. Rather than nurturing his creation, Victor abandons it. We watch with a mix of sadness and horror as the monster wreaks havoc on Victor's life, destroying his family and eventually, on his wedding night, his new bride. Victor chases his monster across the vast, frozen wastelands of the Arctic in a vain attempt to catch him, losing his life before he is able to exact vengeance on the monster he has made. It's not a story that will give you the warm fuzzies. But it does make a simple point: we *create* our own monsters. And once we make them, we must deal with them.

As you seek to be a local church involved in God's mission in the world, you will quickly be confronted with a monster. Unlike

Shelley's monster, he is quite real. He will confront you as you work to bring transformation to marginalized communities, both locally and abroad. This monster is strong, powerful, and (picture a wild-eyed mad scientist screaming) "He's alive!" His name is dependency.

The monster of dependency will ask us how much we can pay rather than how much we can build capacity. He will want you to focus on the condition of your stuff—resources, money, people—rather than the condition of your heart. He will ask you what you can continue to give rather than what you will leave behind, the work that will last, even when you are no longer there. He asks what you will do *for* the people rather than what you can do *with* them.

Dependency has been known by several other names: paternalism, pipelining, imperialism, and false charity. He drives "needy" people to look for a handout, instead of a hand up. He drives the rich to give so they can release their guilt or improve their image—"Look how generous, compassionate, and socially conscious I am!" He attacks those who aren't content with simplistic, easy solutions to problems, who are attempting anything of real and lasting value. We can tell you from firsthand experience, fighting this monster is not easy. And here's the worst part: Dependency is a monster we have made. Some churches and ministries continue to feed him and give him strength. There is a long tradition of complicated, resource-driven dependency flowing from "the rich" to "the poor." We have made this monster and we continue to feed him, and if we're not aware of him, he'll defeat us.

Over the last forty years, with the rise in volunteerism and short-term mission through the local church, millions of people have been mobilized. This movement has had an amazing impact on a sleepy Western church, awakening millions of hearts. In fact, as we've shared, we are among those who were awakened on short-term, volunteer trips. Thoughtful reflection on the problems associated with short-term missions reveals, however, that much of what we've done has not added sustained value. Short-term trips and projects often have short-term goals; they don't build lasting capacity into "the poor" people we serve. Too often, churches have an amazing mission experience, but it comes at the cost of added dependency for the very people they have come to serve. In other words, though our intentions are good, we end up using the poor we serve as means to an end—providing a life-changing experience for us.

To illustrate this, we share a story from some friends who work with a network of believers and local churches in a West African country. Carefully avoiding the monster of dependency, they had begun a number of successful ministries: literacy classes, self-help savings groups, and classes on health and hygiene. These things, within the context of the gospel, were watering the seeds of community transformation. Then a leading church from the United States sent a "trained" team to work in one of the clinics. The team considered the trip a great success, but after they left to head home, our friends working in the country had to shut down the ongoing work to focus on damage control. Why?

With good intentions, the US church brought with them all sorts of bells and whistles to give to the people: toys and T-shirts, trinkets and gifts. They handed out Bibles and books by the hundreds, bought all sorts of food and supplies for the people, and created all sorts of material incentives to get the people to do what they wanted them to do. After they left, our friends went back to the successful initiatives that had begun prior to the visit from the short-term team from the US. They found that the people had changed. "Why don't *you* give us toys and trinkets?" the people began to complain. "We ate better when they came."

When our friends tried to explain that the visit was a special event, and that they were attempting to help the people learn how to sustain themselves long-term, the people responded, "Why don't you just see if you can get more groups like those to come and visit us more often? If they do, we'll do what they tell us, and then there will be no need for us to go through all of the classes you have been teaching us. Why don't you spend your time finding more groups rather than teaching your classes?"

Sadly, our friends eventually had to end their field operations in that region. The visit from that one short-term team had created unsustainable expectations from that community. From that point forward, whenever new groups came in, the first question would be, "What kind of things are *you* going to give us?" rather than "How are you going to help us care for ourselves as equals in the kingdom of God?" The monster had been set loose and it was wreaking havoc.

We want to be very careful, at this point, to make a critical point of distinction. The monster we are talking about is the system of dependency, not the people themselves. Our brothers and sisters who succumb to the allure of dependency are not the monster. Neither are those who go to help. Often the needs are real and the intent to help is genuine, but the solutions are short-term. Dependency does not lead to growth. The challenge for the church is to avoid the trap of dependency and become a champion of authentic, grace-filled transformation. So how do we do something that will help rather than harm the people we seek to serve? For starters, we must recognize that dependency is the result of relationships gone bad. We don't want to kill the relationships. We need to learn how to transition them from dependency-based relationships back to independence (where they don't need us at all), and then to the goal of interdependence (where we join together to bring the kingdom to another community). God's vision for his global glory is the interdependence of his people, using their gifts and resources to serve one another in love. So how do we move toward this type of interdependent friendship?

RELIEF VERSUS DEVELOPMENT

The first step toward friendship and interdependence is understanding the difference between relief and development. *Relief* is when we do something *to* and *for* people. *Development* is when we do something *with* people in a way so they learn to do it for themselves. This is not either-or, doing one or the other. There are certainly times when relief is the right way to respond. When a tsunami wipes away a quarter million lives, the last thing an affected family needs is someone asking them how we can work to ensure long-term economic viability, job-skills training, and literacy initiatives over the course of the next decade. At that moment, they simply need a short-term solution—help finding their missing sixteen-year-old daughter who has just been swept out to sea. They need access to clean water, food, basic shelter, and medical attention. They need immediate relief.

On the other hand, there is a temptation to offer relief when we should be doing development. This ends up hurting the very people we are trying to help. In their book *When Helping Hurts*, authors Steve Corbett and Brian Fikkert agree: "One of the biggest mistakes that North American churches make—by far—is in applying relief in situations in which rehabilitation or development is the appropriate intervention."[1] As we saw in our short-term mission illustration, this approach creates a state of dependency, short-circuiting solutions that might arise from the indigenous leadership, and it further marginalizes the poor. And this is not something unique to the church. It's problematic all over the developing world. Both the government and the church have a long history of paternalism that leads people to believe they cannot do anything without the help of money and resources from others. We need both relief and development, but in the proper balance and in the right context. So what does that look like?

We believe Micah 6:8 provides us with guidance for a balanced response to the needs of people: "He has showed you, O mortal, what is good. And what does the LORD require of you? To act justly and to love mercy and to walk humbly with your God." We are told to walk humbly with God. What does that look like, exactly? For one, it means that we "love mercy." We must have merciful hearts that are eager to help people, that are willing to sacrifice to serve people when they are in need. Our love of showing mercy addresses the short-term problems of poverty. We offer relief by addressing the symptoms of poverty—we give immediate help and assistance. But balanced with our merciful assistance is a love for justice. Acting justly, we address the systems that cause the symptoms. This is the work of development. Without ignoring the symptoms of poverty, it looks beyond them to the root causes—the entrenched habits, patterns, and institutions of the culture that keep people enslaved to the cycle of poverty.

As we were wrestling with all of this in our early days, trying to figure out how to move forward into development work, our friends at World Relief were very helpful, especially our friend and mentor, Don Golden. According to Don, engaging any community that is struggling to achieve their own transformation is a series of steps, a process that leads them away from relief to development. Relief-to-development strategies done well will typically exhibit four stages of operation. This isn't something we've come up with. Any community development specialist will tell you that this is basic Community Development 101. The four phases are as follows (fig. 9.1):

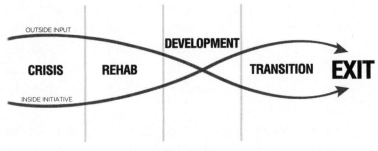

Figure 9.1

1. *Crisis/Relief.* In the first stage, immediate intervention is required. This involves emergency medical care; provision of basic food, water, and clothing; and assurance of safety. This

stage definitely emphasizes the rescue of a community from an active disaster or threat.

2. *Rehabilitation.* In this stage, people are moved from crisis mode to more permanent concerns such as safe, decent housing; clean water and sanitation; and regular access to food and medical care. You might say that in many instances, this is a return to the pre-crisis status quo.

3. *Development.* In this stage, plans are made to move the community forward into economic viability, job development, health education, literacy, agriculture, food security, and so forth. The community moves forward into a way of life where they are more independent of the outside intervention that is necessary in the first two stages.

4. *Sustainability/Transition.* In the final stage, a community is able to sustain its own momentum toward growth and self-sufficiency. The partners gradually remove themselves. The community becomes the model and trainer for another community in need. This stage is only possible when what outside partners do is viewed as temporary from the very beginning. Through the process of development, the community discovers their own dignity, capacity, potential, and power.

When churches fail to plan for a process that will lead to sustainability, they end up putting the community in danger of succumbing to the monster of dependency. To give an illustration, it's like loading everyone onto a plane and then taking off with no idea how to land the plane. Sadly, this describes most of the mission engagement of the church today.

How can you tell if you're stuck in the relief cycle? If your outside intervention continues to either increase or stay the same over time, you're stuck. If local initiative isn't continually rising, you're stuck. In a healthy cycle, outside intervention will decrease over time as local initiative increases.

SINGULAR VERSUS STRATIFIED DEVELOPMENT

As you can imagine, there are different ways to approach development. We break them down into two approaches we call the *singular* and *stratified* development methods. We suggest these as a simple way for church leaders to grasp some basic methodology for development work. We'll start with what these two approaches have in common. Both methods focus on impacting four key distinctives of every community: results, behaviors, values, and beliefs. Stephan Bauman, the CEO of World Relief, defines these as the different levels of the "transformation tree" (fig. 9.2). All of these levels must be understood and addressed in order for any real development to occur in a given context.

RESULTS: WHAT IS SEEN

BEHAVIOR: WHAT IS DONE

VALUES: WHAT IS BEST

BELIEFS: WHAT IS TRUE

Figure 9.2

Beliefs (What is true). All manifestations in a culture or community essentially come from core beliefs. These beliefs shape the perspective from which someone views and perceives their world. They are the roots of the transformation tree.

Values (What is best). Stemming from the core beliefs are values. These are the general shared ideals of the community about what is good or best and what is not. Values are the supporting structure that forms the trunk of the transformation tree.

Behavior (What is done). Individual behaviors are the result of values, which are grounded in beliefs. They are the branches of the transformation tree.

Results (What is seen). Behaviors will manifest outcomes. These outcomes are the results. They are the visible fruit of the transformation tree. The results are the most obvious symptoms that an outsider identifies in a given community.

Efforts to bring change must penetrate all four levels or the changes will not be lasting. Our default tendency is to focus on results. But it's relatively easy to manage or modify behaviors by applying pressure or rewards to get new results. The problem is that once that pressure or incentive is removed, the results disappear. Then, to keep the results, outside pressure must continue to be maintained. This is the monster of dependency.

But why is this true? Because lasting change does not come by simply modifying behaviors. It comes when beliefs and values are also altered. If we never address the heart motivation—the beliefs and values that lie behind our behaviors—we end up simply changing behavior through outside pressure. All good development work recognizes that you need to address all four levels of the transformation tree.

Singular Development: All for One, and One for All!

Singular development strategies (sometimes called "single-point development strategies") take a single key issue and use it as a pinion point for development in a community. This approach is easy to remember if you associate it with the infamous Three Musketeers' battle cry, "All for one, and one for all!" Singular development strategies rally around one key objective and drive it as deeply as possible across the levels of the transformation tree—results, behaviors, values, and beliefs (fig. 9.3). These strategies tend to be very focused and have a high-quality level of impact in a single area. When an organization says, "We drilled ten thousand wells in Africa last year," they really mean it. Singular development strategies provide easy handholds for donors and local churches. If your passion is drilling wells in Africa, you can certainly find a singular development organization that specializes in just that, and they will be happy to have you on board!

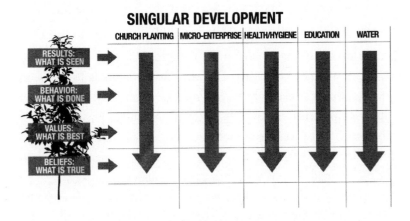

SINGULAR DEVELOPMENT

	CHURCH PLANTING	MICRO-ENTERPRISE	HEALTH/HYGIENE	EDUCATION	WATER
RESULTS: WHAT IS SEEN					
BEHAVIOR: WHAT IS DONE					
VALUES: WHAT IS BEST					
BELIEFS: WHAT IS TRUE					

Figure 9.3

The downside to singular development is that those who use this strategy tend to view all other development in the community through the lens of the single issue they have chosen to focus on. As the old saying goes, "When all you have is a hammer, the whole world is a nail." We don't wish to trivialize the work of those who engage in singular development initiatives. In fact, we celebrate their work. In practice, however, we have seen that no single issue is a silver bullet to fell the giant of poverty in any community. No single issue can address the complex web of issues that cause poverty in the first place. So the solutions offered by singular development are always limited.

For instance, while visiting church planters associated with the ONE Prayer Network throughout Cambodia, I (Jack) personally learned of a singular development initiative that had delivered clean water to a village, but the people there were still suffering from malnutrition. In another village, there was a singular development initiative helping people with food and agriculture, but no one in the village was able to read. And in yet another village, a singular initiative provided literacy classes, but the people were still dying from water-borne illnesses. Each of these singular development initiatives were good for what they sought to address, but they missed the larger goal of total community transformation.

Singular initiatives are often attractive to local churches because they are easy to "take to market" with the congregation. We've noticed that water issues have become very "sexy" for local churches over the last couple years. And to be clear: we're all for water initiatives! But community transformation is never as simple as digging a well. You need to address multiple interconnected issues in a customized way to see real, lasting transformation in a community.

Stratified Development: If One Goes, We All Go!

By contrast, stratified development strategies engage multiple issues simultaneously in a given community (fig. 9.4). In each context (a village or a neighborhood), a sequenced plan is developed that moves progressively deeper over time into all four levels of the transformation tree. At the same time, however, it moves across multiple areas of intervention. As churches utilize this strategy to engage in God's mission, we want to stress that the starting point and foundation for all of this is the local church. The church, along with the local people, becomes the hub from which the community development process grows. Through transformational partnership, the strengths of the indigenous church, the local community, partner agencies, businesses, and the government are all leveraged.

Figure 9.4

If one goes, we all go! Rather than just "doing water," for instance, stratified development will seek to incorporate a plan to solve the water problem along with a handful of other critical interventions. These may include things like microenterprise, job-skill training, housing, education, health/hygiene, and financial literacy. As a result, the community is progressively lifted across a number of areas rather than just one. Issues are solved synergistically, in ever-deepening steps that affect different areas in the life of the community. Critical interventions are identified through a process of community mapping (more on that below).

At the Monroe Circle Community Center, we have multiple initiatives at work simultaneously across the continuum. Every time an individual or family member in the neighborhood interacts with us, it's like a hammer hitting a nail. Each interaction drives deeper the message that they matter to us and matter to God. Not surprisingly, we have begun to call this the "hammer effect." As a family engages with us, these small interventions enter their world at multiple points through their day and week: "You know, this week, my son and daughter came to your Son City Kids program on Sunday afternoon." *Bam!* "Then they came to after-school tutoring every day this week." *Bam!* "I came to GED on Monday night." *Bam!* "And my girlfriend and I both came to The Gathering on Tuesday evening for dinner and to hear Pastor LeRoy speak." *Bam!* "On Thursday afternoon, I came to vocational training to learn about the new construction jobs that are being offered by one of the builders." *Bam!* "On Saturday morning, my girlfriend and kids came to the café to get hot chocolate and pick up a food box to bring home." *Bam!* "When you guys said that you cared about us, you weren't kidding!" *Bam!* Each interaction increases the depth of impact, moving past results to behaviors, past behaviors to values, past values to beliefs.

> Want to see what stratified development looks like in action? Head to *missionalmoves.com* and watch "The Web."

We're big advocates of stratified development strategies. We work across multiple initiatives simultaneously in any community in which we are engaged. Why? We know that over time, we will begin to see the Saved Wholes Gospel permeate not just the results, behaviors, and values of the community, but their core beliefs as well. And when that happens, we begin to see the people we have served in love embrace and champion their own freedom in Christ.

WALKING WITH FRIENDS

If you're tracking thus far, you understand the differences between relief and development, and between singular and stratified development initiatives. Your next question will probably be, "Great ideas, but ... well, how do you do those things?" Do you just start trying things? Do you just assume that all communities are going to need certain basics? Do you ask the people what they think they want or need? We all know that there is usually a huge gap between what people think they need and what they actually do need. So how should you discern what a community needs?

What follows is by no means a magic formula but rather a constantly evolving process. It is certainly easier just to go "drill some wells." If the goal of your mission is for you to feel better about you, then you are probably fine. But if your goal is to actually help a given community, it will require the following kinds of practices:

1. Community Consultation. You will need to start with a small group of indigenous people who are willing to be trained as a team of surveyors to assess and evaluate the community. These are people you already have trusted relationships with. If you don't have those, go back to Missional Move 6 and remember: it all starts with relationships! At this point, you may also need to look for local advocates and experts who understand what community development assessment should include.

2. Community Mapping. This process involves people, even illiterate people, drawing maps of their community and what they dream for it to be. We have examples of community mapping tools that we have used in Monroe Circle and India available at *missional moves.com.*

3. Community Prioritization. Once surveyed, we come alongside our friends in the community to begin to discern the following:

> a. What can they do themselves?
> b. What is the government's responsibility to do?
> c. What things fit neither (a) nor (b) and will require outside help?

This order then sets the sequence for what is done when. The community starts immediately with what it can do. One village in India had issues with malaria due to mosquitoes nesting in stagnant water. The people of the village got out their shovels and dug their own drainage system! Next, we began to equip the local people to access the appropriate governmental support. At times, it is helpful to add our influence so the local people's request is not ignored. In India, this has led to roads being paved, electricity being brought to villages, and local police providing security.

4. Customized Solutions. At this point, we generate a customized stratified development plan for that given environment. Always remember, every community in the world is different. Each is a complicated ecosystem of history, families, culture, and relationships that are interdependent, often in ways that are completely invisible to outsiders. We never assume that a "one size fits all" solution will work in any environment.

5. *Specialized Teams.* We then build teams to engage the key initiatives. These teams meaningfully mobilize our people to work in cooperation with local people to build capacity in them. Now we're back to the demonstration farming model.

6. *Constant Evaluation.* Even after doing all of the above, just because you think something is going to work doesn't mean that it actually will! It may be a fantastic idea, may look great on paper, may be well-supported and even have local buy-in, but for reasons you didn't anticipate, may simply not work. It happens all the time. Rather than being frustrated by it, you simply need to make sure that you build in adequate processes of analysis and evaluation after every initiative to see how each is working.

This is what we call the "development spiral" (fig. 9.5). We start with three turnings of survey (consulation, community mapping, community prioritization), reassessing at every cycle. Then and only then do we actually roll out a prototype program. After more assessment, this leads to a version 2.0, another prototype. Finally, after more assessment, we are ready to actually launch a program. The process of the development spiral is critical because this is where trust and ownership are built with the community with which you

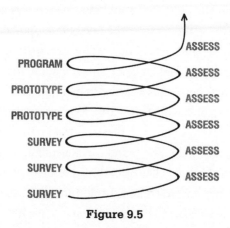

Figure 9.5

are working. Furthermore, in terms of spiritual development, we are modeling for the entire community a grace-based process of confession and repentance by which we become more like Jesus.

THE POWER OF CHOICE

We started this chapter with the story of the monster's success. But what happens to the monster of dependency when you make the missional move from relief to development? We think the story of Manju is a great illustration of the result (you can watch a video of Manju's story at *missionalmoves.com*):

"A choice is a funny thing. It seems insignificant until all of your choices are taken from you. What would you do if all of your choices were predetermined for you? My name is Manju, and I am sixteen years old. I cannot choose to go to school. I cannot choose what to wear. I cannot even choose what I will eat.

"My day starts the same way every day. I wake up when the goats are ready to go out to pasture, and I sit with them in the scorching hot sun for ten hours. I don't get paid a wage until one of the goats gives birth to twins. If no goat has twins, my family will go hungry.

"Last summer, I was shepherding goats and not a single one of them gave birth to twins. I was beaten for this, and told I was a bad daughter for not providing for my family. I began to think to myself that if this was the only life I could ever lead, it was not worth living. Every day was the same as the one before. One day I ran from my mother to the outskirts of our village to a dusty field and chose to do the one thing I had a choice about. I ate berries from a bush that I knew were poisonous in order to end my life. I ate as many as I could in hopes of leaving this world. Everything went dark.

"My friend found me lying there on the ground and rushed to the village to seek help. She found Mr. Rajendran, who carried me in his car to the hospital. The next thing I remember seeing was Mr. Rajendran in my hospital room. I told him that I did not want to continue living because there was nothing to live for.

"Mr. Rajendran told me of a man-God that I had never heard of before. He talked to me about Jesus who came and lived among us to provide us with a life of meaning and purpose. He said that Jesus came to give us a life filled with hope for now and hope for the future.

"Soon after this I met a team of people from Granger. They were a new kind of people for me. They were like Mr. Rajendran in the way that they cared for us and treated one another. They had light skin and strange words. They talked to us about Jesus, who had sent them from a great distance to come and serve him and the people of my village.

"I also learned of a man named Pastor Sam [a church planter Granger has trained] who was a shepherd like me, only he is a shepherd for the souls of men. I learned that Jesus was a man who loves us, not like the other gods who are cold and uncaring.

"In my culture there are many gods. They rule over everything and demand our devotion. From Pastor Sam, Mr. Rajendran, and the Granger teams, I have learned that Jesus loves us like we are little children, as a shepherd cares for his flock.

"This year in Pastor Sam's church, my mother and I decided to put away our other gods and only follow Jesus. For the first time ever in my life I am beginning to have choices. My mother and I have chosen to improve our relationship based on what we are learning from Pastor Sam.

"I am now taking sewing classes in the evenings when I return from the fields. I am hoping that one day I will be able to become a tailor so that I can provide a better wage for my family. I have seen how the Christian men and women who are married treat one another. Next year when I am given to a husband, I am requesting that my mother choose a Christian man so that we can follow Jesus together.

"The people of Granger Church have worked alongside our people to bring many changes to our village. My family and I now live in a new home, instead of a hut. A new well provides clean water. The children in our village attend school for the first time ever. They have even come to my village to teach the children English so the children can get good jobs in the big cities or go to college one day.

"In choosing to follow Jesus, I am beginning to see a new world. It is a world of choices. It is a world where other people love and serve one another to provide the kind of place that Jesus said was possible. It is a new world for people like me to find love and purpose. This place is called the kingdom of God. I am seeing it coming here and now in my village every day."

Chapter 10

FROM PROFESSIONALS TO FULL PARTICIPATION
Missional Move 10

Recently, my (Jack) son asked me what it takes to join one of the Special Forces programs of the armed services. I could tell there was more to his inquiry than mere academic interest. As a great admirer of our nation's armed forces, I was more than ready to answer! I talked about the extraordinary commitment, courage, and strength of mind and body necessary to even qualify for such programs, much less graduate from them. I described with growing excitement the types of extreme missions such individuals are regularly tasked to carry out. As I talked, I saw his face turn from eager attentiveness to discouragement and defeat. By the time I stopped to take a breath, he was deep in contemplation. I asked him what he was thinking, and he responded with childlike candor, "Well, I thought maybe it might be cool to be part of something like that someday. But honestly, it just sounds too hard." Obviously, I'm not a great motivational speaker!

Unfortunately, many people in our churches feel just like my son. They live with a perception that being fully engaged in the mission of God is too hard. It's something that a staff member or an experienced volunteer can do, but you have to be slightly crazy. We call this the "commando Christian fallacy," and it's alive and well in most of our churches today.

I (Jack) saw this firsthand when I came on staff at Granger. I spoke with several eager potential volunteers about opportunities to serve. I'd say something like, "I'm so glad that you've offered to help! Can you volunteer every Sunday from 2 to 6 p.m. to work in a gang-infested inner-city neighborhood with children from some of the most abusive, dysfunctional, and broken families in our community? Many will have drug or alcohol problems by the time they are twelve. Many will have significant behavioral, attention deficit, or learning disorders. So ... are you in?" Like my son, many would tell me, in so many words, "Well, I thought maybe it might be cool to be part of something like that. But honestly, it just sounds too hard."

When we took a closer look, we began to notice that the people who served on our teams outside the walls of our church actually were commando Christians. There was a comparatively small handful of committed men, women, and students who did everything! The same group was traveling to India, serving in our community center, and involved in many of the opportunities we offered. So why were so few stepping out?

We started taking informal surveys among people who weren't plugged in to our mission programs. It soon became clear that the primary barriers were fear and busyness. We could have tried shaming people, saying, "Suck it up. Get over it. Get moving. If you really love Jesus ..." But real servant leadership requires that we meet people where they are, helping to remove barriers so they can move forward. So the question for us became, "How can we meet people where they are and help them take small steps forward on mission, overcoming their fear and busyness?"

The truth is that people in your church will not just fling themselves full bore into a missional lifestyle. They will need to start with small steps of missional activity. That was our goal, so we decided to create a series of steps that would progressively move people forward from occasional *activities* toward a missional *lifestyle*. At the time, the only opportunities we had provided required long-term involvement in a team. But for most people, this was too big of a first step. That's when we realized we needed to expand our spectrum of involvement.

THE SPECTRUM OF INVOLVEMENT

Acts 1:8 was already our basic framework for mobilizing our people locally (i.e., Jerusalem), regionally (i.e., Judea), internationally (i.e., ends of the earth), and cross-culturally (i.e., Samaria). Since a cross-cultural experience can happen at any of those places, we intentionally kept Samaria apart, as an overarching value to guide the other three. Within each geographic locus we began to organize opportunities into steps that were accessible, "chewable," and progressive. We wouldn't start by asking people to swim across the English Channel; we'd ask them to get into the pool. Eventually, they would be ready for a swim across the lake. And at some point, with enough practice swimming, they could tackle the channel.

We called this our spectrum of involvement (fig. 10.1). In each geographic locus, we built a series of steps, starting with access, moving to project, then ongoing teams, and finally leadership.

Access Events: Keeping It Sassy!

Based on responses from people who were not serving, we realized quickly that whatever we offered as the lowest possible point of entry would need to honor a handful of nonnegotiable values. We simply tell people that we need to keep these access events "SASsy": simple, accessible, and scalable.

	ACCESS MINISTRY	PROJECT MINISTRY	ONGOING TEAMS	LEADERSHIP
LOCAL				
REGIONAL				
INTERNATIONAL				

CROSS-CULTURAL

Figure 10.1

- *Simple.* Anytime we offer an access event, it needs to be simple enough that anyone can do it. It cannot require that people be skilled carpenters or EMTs, know how to program computers or even hang drywall.
- *Accessible.* An access event needs to provide participation for everyone regardless of age, gender, or spiritual status. To the degree that is possible, all of our access events are family friendly (except every now and then, we will reserve an opportunity that does not include children simply because some people don't like children much and/or would rather work without having them around), age appropriate, and open to believers and nonbelievers alike.
- *Scalable.* For every access event, we have to either spin up or cycle down to accommodate however many and whoever shows up. People have some measure of tolerance for an event being poorly organized. They have zero tolerance for showing up and not being needed. Access events guarantee that everyone can participate, regardless of how many or how few attend.

One past example of a local access event at Granger is what we call our Second Saturday experience. Begun in 2005 after developing our Spectrum of Involvement, we designed Second Saturday to counter every objection that we reasonably heard as to why people did not or could not serve. Second Saturday (as the name suggests) occurs every month on the second Saturday of the month in order to eliminate questions or confusion about when it occurs. Rather than showing up at service opportunities, we ask that volunteers simply come to the Granger church campus by 8:30 a.m. After a ten-minute briefing, we then dismiss them to the parking lot where rented school buses are waiting to take them to various service projects around the community. As often as possible, we connect the access projects with ongoing teams.

SECOND SATURDAY AT GRANGER

Want to see how Second Saturday is done at Granger? Head to *missionalmoves.com* and watch the video titled "Second Saturday."

This provides the ongoing team with a huge infusion of manpower to accomplish their mission and also exposes new people to the work of that team. As new people serve alongside ongoing teams, people experience firsthand what it would look like to serve with that team, without any pressure to commit yet.

All serving opportunities are geared for the lowest skill level. After two and a half hours of meaningful service, the buses arrive again at each site and load the volunteers back up, thus meeting our guaranteed promise that people will be back on campus by noon. We do not take attendance, we do not require preregistration, and we do not require that volunteers bring special tools, clothing, or skills. This ministry has been incredibly effective over the past six years, and through it, we have seen a cumulative mobilization of thousands. In addition, at each Second Saturday briefing, we always ask who is serving for the first time, and almost always find that at least 50 percent or more of those present have never served outside the walls of the church before.

Project Ministries: Low Risk, High Effect

Access events cannot be an end unto themselves. When people have a desire to go deeper or connect further, we need an infrastructure to answer that call. Without that, serving becomes less of an entry into deeper and deeper opportunities of commitment and enrichment, and more of a guilt-relief valve that needs to be tapped periodically to assure us that a requirement has been met to "do *something*" missional.

Access events and experiences need to pour into something beyond themselves. Simultaneously, these next steps cannot feel too far removed from the relatively low-risk, low-commitment ease of the access experience. That next step beyond is project ministries and opportunities.

Like access experiences, project opportunities allow people to experiment with given ministry types, locations, and environments without requiring them to sign on for ongoing teams who will depend on their regular involvement. Project opportunities are governed by three simple parameters:

1. *Limited Time.* Project opportunities will state a fixed start and stop point for their function and will almost never surpass seventy-two hours. Most will happen over a half day, a single day, a long weekend, or in shifts around a particular event.

2. *Limited Scope.* As with access experiences, projects will seek to keep activity and experiences on a level where most people feel comfortable interacting. They are seeking a deeper and richer experience beyond the taste of what they experience during access events, but overloading them too soon is still a risk. As a result, limiting the scope of project ministries is critical and advisable.

3. *Limited Commitment.* At the project level, certain things are necessarily occurring that are absent at the access level. Leaders may require registration, small fees to cover transportation or food, and permission forms or other infrastructure necessities that are unnecessary at the access level (where the highest degree of anonymity and lowest possible barrier to entry are the name of the game).

In 2006, as we were attempting to renovate our Monroe Circle Community Center in downtown South Bend, we hosted several all-weekend builds that lasted seventy-two hours. We engaged our already committed construction team members and leaders (ongoing teams and core leadership). We had primed interest in the builds by aligning several Second Saturdays (access opportunities) around smaller projects at the site throughout the year. As a result, when it came time to destroy the interior and replace the entire facing of the center, volunteers who had experimented at the access level were given a project opportunity to wade in a step further for a half-day shift. In addition, Granger's Student and College Ministries bundled project opportunities alongside the event. The collective impact was massive as hundreds of volunteers were mobilized across the entire spectrum of involvement. All stages of the spectrum were energized by the experience, but those at the project level were particularly moved to see what can be accomplished with just a little more effort beyond the access stage.

Monroe Circle Community Center (before)

Monroe Circle Community Center (after)

It was an extraordinary experience that taught us a critical lesson about the power of project-oriented thinking, especially when it is well-connected beforehand with access events and afterward with ongoing teams. As a testimony to the overall collaborative effect of a fully mobilized spectrum of involvement, the end product that now stands as the Monroe Circle Community Center is approximately a $1.5 million structure. All but about 30 percent of the labor to renovate the entire facility was provided by the volunteer hours of men, women, students, and families of Granger Community Church through the entire spectrum of involvement. That cut the actual dollar expenditure necessary to just a little more than $500,000.

Ongoing Teams: The Backbone

As one moves from the left side of the spectrum toward ongoing teams and leadership, by nature, the commitment at all levels increases. While a person who does not yet have a committed relationship to Jesus is welcome to participate at the access and project levels, people functioning at the ongoing team level will in some cases need to be devoted followers of Christ.

Ongoing teams are the backbone around which all other elements of the spectrum of involvement hold together. Without the stable, on-the-ground presence of the people of God in the given contexts, the mission loses its incarnational grounding and the possibility of real transformation. Jesus didn't commute; he came and "dwelt" among us. Ongoing teams keep it real, lasting, and incarnational. Access participants may never come back. Neither may project participants. But ongoing teams "dwell," and this promise of traction and presence develops and transforms communities.

Therefore, ongoing teams are carefully maintained, mentored, and celebrated. We try hard to ensure that ongoing teams are decentralized (i.e., having the freedom to live out their mission as best they see fit within their context) and yet centrally recognized, respected, and discipled to stay healthy. The health of ongoing teams is encouraged through the following:

- *Fixed Terms.* Even at this level, individuals need to believe that there is both a way in and a way out. We try to encourage ministry cycles that fall in line with natural rhythms, such as school years, to give people easily identified cycles of service.
- *Fortified.* We have observed that people who function at the ongoing team level really want a deeper level of commitment and input from staff, staff structure, and volunteer leadership that reflects their commitment to the ministry of the church at large. As a result, we regularly purchase and distribute books, foster discussions on both strategic and tactical considerations, record simple podcasts or CD-based messages specific to issues that they are addressing, build Facebook or online community pages to facilitate interaction and education, encourage feedback loops to a variety of questions and ongoing concerns, and meet team members for lunch or coffee to ensure that they stay in a state of both actual and perceived contact to both their team leaders and those of us who serve them as their staff leaders.

- *Fun.* We get that, as Christians, we're fighting a battle against evil in all its forms. That's just plain hard. Yet we believe joy is available at all times. If the life of a team doesn't involve joy and fun, it becomes an obligation or a martyrdom opportunity. But when the teams stay fun and joyful, momentum flows freely. We want our people serving alongside people they enjoy, experiencing the joy only the gospel gives. This environment creates the kind of glue necessary for effective ongoing teams.

As the spectrum of involvement operates, access and project participants get to see firsthand what the ongoing teams do on a regular basis, and the ongoing teams receive a booster shot of volunteer labor that can help them to do things they might struggle to do on their own.

Leadership: A Time and Place for Commandos

It has been stated many times, "Everything rises and falls on leadership." The simple reality is that in any church larger than just a few dozen people, leadership structures must be in place to guarantee growth and health. Leaders are absolutely essential. The bigger and more aggressive your organization, the more valuable they become. In local churches seeking to have every member mobilized on mission, leadership is your most important resource.

We want to dispel the commando Christian fallacy. But make no mistake; there are people who have God-given uncanny capacity in terms of the leadership. To further develop the people who lead the ongoing teams, we spend a significant amount of time ensuring that they receive the following:

- *Fractal Leadership.* Organic church guru Neil Cole, in his book *Organic Church*, describes a method of leadership theory that he calls "Fractal Leadership."[1] While we will discuss this idea in greater detail in the next chapter (Missional Move 11), it is relevant here to simply state that a fractal is the simplest possible repeating pattern in any system. You might also call this your DNA, or the minimum arrangement of core elements that define your church. If you hold tightly to a very small set of core (and fractal) values, you do not have to intensively manage the manifestations beyond the values themselves. It took us years to figure out how to boil our values down to something that could be communicated quickly and effectively, but now we can relay them to any leader in as little as ten minutes, or as long as several days. But once the leader owns the "fractal," they can make it so in their context without us micromanaging them.

- *Delegated Authority.* It amazes some people when we tell them that our Son City Kids team leader (who is an unpaid volunteer) has budget authority over a $20,000 budget. Why? Most churches don't really delegate authority or foster independence; rather, they maintain control and foster codependency. If we are confident that the leader is holding to our DNA, then we are confident that they are better informed about spending decisions in their target context than we are. The result has been that some of our most innovative ideas have surfaced from within our ranks rather than from above them. Captain D. Michael Abrashoff's experience mirrors this concept in his book *It's Your Ship*, which recounts the management strategies he learned as the senior officer aboard the United States Navy's USS *Benfold* combat vessel. He writes: "The command-and-control approach [to leadership] is far from the most efficient way to tap people's intelligence and skills. To the contrary, I found that the more control I gave up, the more command I got. In the beginning, people kept asking my permission to do things. Eventually, I told the crew, 'It's *your* ship. You're responsible for it. Make a decision and see what happens.' ... Show me an organization in which employees take ownership, and I will show you one that beats its competitors."[2]

- *Centralized Support.* Our leaders know: try, experiment, try harder and even fail, but do not hold position. The war for the souls of men and women in our world will not be won by a force that is not daily gaining ground. And we mean that. They also know, "We have your back." We constantly reiterate, "If you sound for the cavalry, plan on us showing up!"

I once worked in an organization where if I got in over my head, I could be assured that I would be the only one who would drown. Many others have been there as well. There is no cavalry to call. There is no one who shows up if you're backed into a corner. Real community transformation is bloody, sweaty, dirty, and gritty. It requires patience, courage, and more than just a little audacity. As a result, leaders not only have to have the freedom to do those things but they also need to know if they get in over their heads, you will show up in force.

A FINAL WORD

As a final point, we'd like to say our goal is not to push for a specific program, like Second Saturday, although that has been a helpful tool for many other churches. The specifics of our events are not the point. We ruthlessly employ a system of ongoing evaluation to keep us focused on the principles behind the spectrum, not the specific programs.

The ultimate point of this missional move is to get you thinking in terms of how to move your people out of their seats and into the Story in a series of steps. People in our churches want to make a

CONSTANT EVALUATION

We're actually in the process of rebooting the entire way the spectrum will play out in our life together at Granger right now. Curious to learn more? Visit *missionalmoves.com* and look for the ebook *Spectrum of Involvement: Going 3D and Surfing the Wave.* We also have some great videos available where you can see what some of our various access, project, and team initiatives look like.

difference. They want to be part of what God is doing in the world. They just have no idea how to start, where to go, or what to do in order to walk down that path. As you make this missional move, we believe that you will be astounded at the surge of God's people taking part in the mission of God in the world.

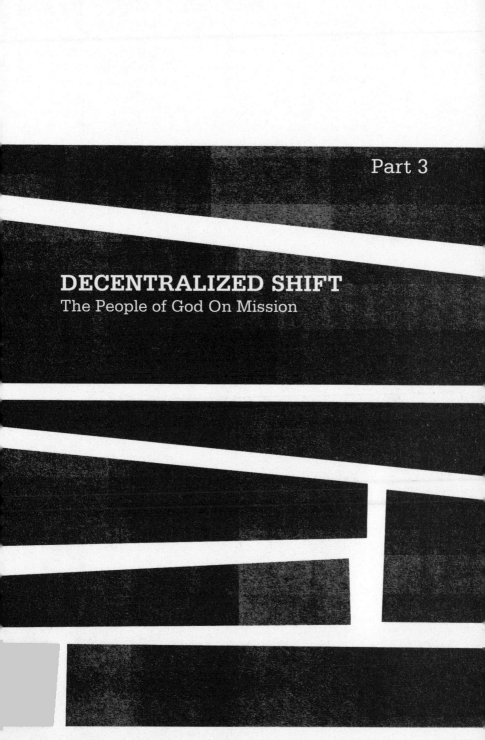

Part 3

DECENTRALIZED SHIFT
The People of God On Mission

In the last section, we rediscovered that the local church is designed by God to be the hub for transformation in any neighborhood, village, or city. We're hoping that you've been flooded with new tactical ideas for how to unleash that transformation in the place where God has planted your church. Take a minute, before starting the next section, to sift through all the good ideas and try to find the one "God idea" you need to focus on. As you look over the last five missional moves, where do you see God already prompting, working, and leading forward your local church? That's the God idea. Keeping in mind the ideas presented in the second section, ask yourself, "What is the God idea for our local church? How can we join him?"

Organized local churches create a network of sustainability for kingdom work over the long haul. In order for your local church to be effective, it has to have a laser-focused vision. However, God's desire is to birth a vision not only inside every local church, but also inside *every single follower of Jesus*.

In part 2, "Centralized Shift," we focused on how to mobilize people around the centralized vision of your local church. In this next section, "Decentralized Shift," we'll look at how to release and equip your people for the unique vision God has created for them. Much of that will fall outside of the organized, budgeted, and staffled initiatives of your local church. Sound like a recipe for conflict or chaos? We hear your concern, but you may have already noticed a growing restlessness in your people. Growing numbers of believers don't just want to plug in to the preexisting options we've created. God is calling them to something else. Now is the time to release the people of God on mission. Ultimately, Jesus designed the church to be a grassroots movement.

Decentralized Shift

11. From Formal to Fractal Leadership
12. From Institution to Movement
13. From Mega and Multi to Mega, Multi, and Micro
14. From "We Can Do It; You Can Help" to "You Can Do It; We Can Help"
15. From Great Commission to Great Completion

Chapter 11

FROM FORMAL TO FRACTAL LEADERSHIP

Missional Move 11

One of the best leadership books we've read in the past decade is Rod Beckstrom and Ori Braffman's *The Starfish and the Spider: The Unstoppable Power of Leaderless Organizations*. In it the authors posit two different types of organizations: the spider and the starfish.

If you look at a spider and a starfish, they share similarities. They both have bodies with appendages that sprout outward from a radial center. Yet even though they appear quite similar in some ways, there are big differences between them. If you cut the head off of a spider, you kill the entire organism. A spider organization is one where you have a standard hierarchy, a "central brain" or decision-making body that regulates the actions of the organization directly. If something destroys the decision-making body (i.e., cutting off the head), the entire organization dies.

Starfish do not have this problem. If you cut a starfish in half, what happens? You get two starfish. In each of its cells, a starfish

Figure 11.1

has all that it needs to completely regenerate a completely new starfish. Starfish organizations, unlike spider organizations, make sure they have everything they need to reproduce in every cell of their organization.

Rarely, however, are we able to choose between these two extremes: the spider or the starfish. We realized that our unique challenges at Granger required a hybrid. Could we become a *spiderfish?*

We went looking for this hybrid model because we are an organized megachurch that wants to unleash autonomous, viral movements. We are committed to being attractional and missional, organizational and autonomous. We want the power a centralized structure brings to shared vision and shared resources, while simultaneously cultivating the kind of decentralized movements that no longer depend upon "headquarters" to completely feed, fund, or regulate what they do. Over the last decade, we've been progressively transitioning into a new way of describing and implementing this hybrid leadership style. We call it *fractal leadership.*

FRACTALS: A DEFINITION
We owe a debt of gratitude to Neil Cole[1] and Wayne Cordeiro,[2] whose initial insights on the connection between fractal geometry

and the realm of leadership inspired our own reflection on this subject. A fractal is the smallest repeatable pattern of any given system. It might be a mathematical system, a biological system, or a social system, but whatever system you are dealing with, a fractal is the part of that system that is simple and repeatable. The simpler and more easily repeatable a fractal is, the harder the system is to break or destroy. The more sophisticated and complex a fractal is, the harder it is to replicate, the easier it is to mutate, and the easier it is to destroy. If I draw a triangle, I'm going to guess you can repeat this simple shape in five seconds flat. That's a simple, repeatable fractal. But if I ask you to recreate the Sistine Chapel, it's not so simple or repeatable. It's not a good fractal.

In nature, fractals are everywhere. They exist in crystals and minerals, plants and animals—things we use and see every day. DNA follows a fractal pattern—it exists in a repeatable, simple form and has everything needed for replication and growth. By extension, fractal leadership is a method of conveying the most critical components of a church and/or movement's mission, vision, and values in such a way that they are:

- *simple* (easily understood),
- *repeatable* (easily communicated),
- *adaptable* (easily deployed into patterns customizable to any environment), and yet
- *consistent* (predictable at a minimum baseline in terms of outcomes).

FRACTAL VERSUS FORMAL: A COMPARISON

We are not saying formal leadership is bad and fractal leadership is good. It's not an either-or choice. It's a both-and. You can be a good formal leader and a bad formal leader. You can be a good fractal leader or a bad fractal leader. In our own journey for the past twenty-five years, we've been employing good formal leadership structures and systems within our teams and environments at Granger. Mark Beeson is a strong, intuitive leader, whose normal style of leadership is a fusion of fractal and formal, a combination that has made the changes described in this book possible. We don't see fractal and formal leadership styles as distinct and unrelated. They exist on a continuum, and the best leaders balance elements of each style. We would encourage you as a church leader to examine your own leadership style to determine where you are on this continuum.

In a formal leadership environment, only the senior leader or a select few leaders at the top of the organization have the whole picture. As figure 11.2 indicates, the top square is invested in the shaded "mission and vision" for the entire organization. In a local church environment, this would typically be the lead pastor, a small management team of pastors, or perhaps the board of elders.

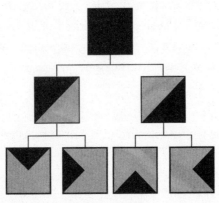

Figure 11.2

As you move down the chain of leadership away from the top level, however, each new level you encounter has less and less of the total vision for the organization. The top leaders do all that they can to keep the organization united, gathering all of the different groups together. If they are effective, there is shared vision across the organization. Each layer of the organization (usually overseen by staff in the local church) manages its "chunk" of the vision and is responsible for ensuring that when the people below them add their piece of the pie, it all adds up and they can make the expected contribution to the level above them. Each individual, then, while they may vaguely be aware of the top-level concerns, really has just enough information and ownership of the overall mission as is needed to do what they need to do.

There are some positives to formal leadership:

- *Alignment.* One of the most amazing things about a local church with great formal leadership is the sense of alignment. When all the various teams and departments assemble into the shape that the visionary pastor originally saw, everyone in the place has a profound sense that "we are better together!"

- *Symmetry and Beauty.* When you watch all those moving parts work together, it's flat-out inspiring and amazing. When the local church is working right, there's nothing else like it. The unity, symmetry, and beauty of that church are winsome to an entire community. We've had more than one pastor ask us, "How do you get all these people to serve at Granger?" We reply, "How do you stop your people from serving?" Give people a clear vision, mission, and values. Help them find their gifts and use them in a team that works in alignment with all the other teams. Do that, and you can't stop people from serving!

- *Great Leaders Emerge.* The larger the box gets, the more working parts and layers you have in the middle. The leadership required at every level just keeps getting higher and higher. So you keep calling out greater and greater leaders. That's good! Ninety percent of our current staff came up through the ranks. That's a sign of leadership health. We have volunteer leaders who run teams that have hundreds of volunteers on them and provide oversight on tens of thousands of dollars. How cool is that?

There are also some challenges that come with formal leadership:

- *Distance.* As the church grows, the challenge is the growing distance between the people down "at the bottom" and the original vision "up at the top." Additional layers need to be added because of growth, which means hierarchies grow. Hierarchy is necessary in formal structures, but it does create distance.
- *Leaks.* Always, there will be a vision leak, values leak, and relational leak as hierarchies are formed.
- *Unintentional Oppression.* Formal leadership inadvertently creates a sense of a caste system, even if everyone in the system is working against it. Why? We are creating multiple layers that—whether we like it or not—leave people out of the game and out of leadership. As layers increase, greater leadership is required at each level. Although that calls out greater leaders, it means fewer people can qualify for a leadership role.

Now what if instead of slicing a core mission into pieces that are further split by people who are increasingly distant from the vision at the top, the leaders give the people the core essentials of the vision necessary to own the vision for themselves. Instead of contributing a piece of the pie so that the top-down vision can be fulfilled, leaders are cut loose from the central authority and empowered to make the vision happen in their own environment.

In formal leadership, the mission is segmented and divided up so that each person offers a unique contribution. The leader says, "We're going to draw a detailed daisy. Person one, you draw the stem; it needs to be green. Person two, you draw the leaf; there can be only one of them. Person three, you draw the petals; they need to be red. Exactly seventeen of them too. Then we'll put it all back together and get our end product. Voila!" Everyone contributes a piece, and all is directed by one key leader.

In fractal leadership, the leader instead says, "We're all going to draw a flower. It needs to have these minimum requirements: a stem,

Figure 11.3

at least one leaf, and petals. Go!" Anything that meets those three criteria is considered a success. It doesn't matter whether you draw a daisy, an orchid, or a delphinium. It doesn't matter whether it's red or blue or white. If it has a stem, leaf, and petals, it's "in." It counts.

Even if, as a leader, I have a red daisy in my head, I may be surprised by the contributions that others bring. I might never have imagined the intricate beauty of a delphinium or an orchid drawn by one of my team members. So fractal leadership is marked by:

- *Decentralized Structure.* No one person is the gatekeeper for the entire mission, and everyone carries all aspects of the mission.
- *Open-Ended Outcomes.* A much broader range of things can be said to "pass inspection."
- *Creativity and Innovation over Conformity and Quality.* Whereas formal leadership requires a predictable product with comfort and assurance every time you experience it, fractal leadership only ensures quality control at the most basic level: the level of the fractal. This leads to amazing innovation and creativity on outcomes.
- *Descriptive Rather Than Prescriptive Processes.* With fractal leadership, the end goal is visualized, along with the necessary fractals to be guarded in moving forward, but there is tremendous freedom in the methodologies employed to do so.

When you see the differences between formal and fractal leadership, it doesn't take long to understand why true movements are almost always fractal rather than formal. It is this fractal form of leadership that has enabled our movement in India. But to make it a bit more tangible, let's look at an example a little closer to home.

FRACTAL LEADERSHIP IN THE REAL WORLD

Since 2002, we have had an event called the Food Drop. This access event, which happens every January, mobilizes more than twenty-five hundred people. In partnership with Feed the Children and a host of additional churches, local agencies, businesses, and not-for-profit entities, we have teams of volunteers off-load (by hand) approximately 225,000 pounds of food and personal care items into smaller trucks and then distribute those resources to more than two dozen drop locations. In one day, we reach five thousand of the most vulnerable individuals and families in our community. Because we have it in January, this event usually coincides with arctic conditions, so we take pride in the turnout of volunteers. The day is successful, not because of all the meticulous and elaborate planning from staff, but because each of the more than 150 volunteer leaders understands and owns the vision and mission of the Food Drop. It's a great example of the spiderfish we talked about earlier—a fusion of formal and fractal leadership. Year after year, the leaders who volunteer for the Food Drop know and understand the core purpose of the event. Beyond that, they have freedom to be creative, improvise, and do what they feel is necessary to make that day a success. Here's the simple, repeatable, adaptable, and consistent fractal we give them for the Food Drop:

- *Opportunity over Efficiency.* Forming human chains across the parking lot is nowhere near as simple as it would be to hire a couple of forklifts and a few pallet jacks and get the job done much faster. But efficiently offloading the boxes is not our value. Rather, efficiently and meaningfully mobilizing twenty-five hundred volunteers is.

- *Adapt, Improvise, and Overcome.* We borrowed this maxim from the United States Marine Corps; "Adapt, improvise, and overcome" is a maxim that understands that even with highly organized events like Food Drop, something always goes wrong or requires some sort of in-the-moment decision. We therefore instill the value at the leadership level to quite simply do whatever is necessary to get the job done.
- *Autonomy within Boundaries.* At the most basic level, we instill in our leaders a core understanding that it's really their show once the trucks leave the parking lot and head to their locations. We require them ahead of time to submit a site plan to us so that we know they have thought through the various details of their drop location, but we do not regulate what that plan needs to be specifically.

The Food Drop in January 2011 happened during the worst blizzard that northern Indiana has experienced in more than thirty years, setting a record for the amount of snowfall received in a twenty-four-hour period (more than thirty-four inches!). The really odd thing was that most of that snowfall happened during our event—from about seven in the morning until about one in the afternoon. While naysayers will most certainly categorize us as crazy or stupid for having proceeded anyway, we were already well underway for the day when the flurries turned from flakes to "falling drifts." Despite the conditions, we still had more than a thousand Granger people arrive to participate with a willingness to move forward into the ever-increasing storm and deliver the much-needed supplies to area families.

INDOMITABLE SNOWMEN (AND WOMEN) ON FILM

If you would like to see the media produced to capture the snow-driven insanity of the 2011 Granger Food Drop, head to *missionalmoves.com* and watch the video "Food Drop."

Though the city of South Bend declared a state of emergency at about 10:00 a.m., teams from our church were already knocking on doors and trudging through snowbanks to deliver supplies to shut-ins who could no longer get out of their driveways. While professional snowplowing services struggled to get their trucks onto the streets, volunteer team leaders recruited vehicles with four-wheel drive and chained snow tires to take loads of boxes and team members into Housing Authority complexes where their larger trucks could not travel or go.

Our teams actually delivered all their boxes within the same timeframe that they usually did during years when the weather was more cooperative. By one o'clock in the afternoon, all teams had radioed in that their sites were complete and that they were heading to get a hot cup of cocoa. As we began to listen to stories, it became evident that the more difficult it became to deliver the boxes, the harder the people worked to engineer solutions to get it done. As staff, we simply sat back and marveled. Our team leaders had truly grasped the core of the mission—the Food Drop fractal.

In a later thank-you note to our team leaders, we told them that we would forever remember them as our "Indomitable Snowmen" (and women!) because they had refused to accept defeat despite the abominable blizzard conditions, instead insisting on pushing ahead to bring the kingdom of God from "up there to down here" where and when it was needed most. As staff, we were surprised at the creativity, ingenuity, and innovation that were displayed to get the job done.

FRACTAL CORE: THE BARE ESSENTIALS

As with the Food Drop, if you want to create a fractal model for leadership at any level, you have to be able to identify what we call your "fractal core." A fractal core is simply the "thing you're trying to replicate." It is the simplest, essential, repeatable set of data that is irreducible for your people. It provides the proverbial line you cannot cross and defines what must be true of any finished product. Fractal leadership that isn't clear about what needs to be replicated won't work. That's why you need a fractal core, and it should be highly customized to the DNA of your local church. Beware of trying to take this core from someone else or "borrowing" it from another leader or church. Define your own, or it won't work for you.

The Seven Metaphors of the Fractal Core at Granger

We have attempted to implement fractal leadership in all our teams "outside the walls," locally and internationally. We have articulated our fractal core through a series of word pictures we call the "seven life mission metaphors." You will notice much of the language in these word pictures mirrors several missional moves. The seven metaphors make some of our key missional moves understandable to people. Each of these word pictures begins with an invitation to "become" something, and each requires a corresponding action.

> We've provided the "elevator speech" for you here, but if you're interested in more details, visit *missionalmoves.com* for an extended cut.

1. Become a Knight: Bringing In the Reign of the King

What was the job of a knight? A knight was the physical presence of the king throughout the realm. The fundamental job of a knight was to bring the will of the king into reality. Our King is benevolent and kind, desiring the whole expression of the gospel. As a result, as agents of the kingdom, we will always be at work for shalom.

Fractal Value: Holism

2. Become a Jedi: Using the Force of the Laser, Not the Flashlight

The more focused a beam of light is, the more powerful it becomes. At Granger, we have decided to be laserlike in our focus. We would rather drill deeply in few places than barely break the surface in many locations.

Fractal Value: Focus

3. Become a Tightrope Walker: Balancing Mobilization with Impact

We are committed to balancing the two goals of (1) mobilizing our people and (2) connecting that mobilization to long-term, sustainable impact. We recognize that sometimes it requires some fancy maneuvering in order to do so (like walking a tightrope).

Fractal Value: Development

4. Become a Highway Planner: Building On-Ramps Rather Than Dead Ends

We are committed to breaking down whatever barriers discourage people's desire to engage the mission of God. So we develop identifiable next steps that meet people wherever they find themselves and help them move toward deeper levels of engagement and commitment.

Fractal Value: Spectrum of Involvement

5. Become a Gardener: Cultivating Grassroots Movements

We want to cultivate and fertilize grassroots movements. We are committed to bottom-up, small, strategic, reproducing interventions.

Fractal Value: Bottom-Up versus Top-Down

6. Become a Cowboy: Committing to Strategic "Pardnerships"

We're not trying to be experts at everything. We refuse to work alone. We will seek to develop meaningful partnership with players from every domain of society in pursuit of a kingdom vision.

Fractal Value: Transformational Partnership

7. Become a Geek: Committing to Leveraging Technology

Technology is a force multiplier. We will leverage technology to multiply our relational connectivity, streamline communication, develop reliable systems, and amplify our message.

Fractal Value: Effectiveness

━━━━ ━━━

Please notice as you look back over the above seven metaphors that they essentially mirror the material that we have been illustrating throughout this book. We can "decompress" them as a whole or in parts to fill a 250-page book, or we can "compress" them into a five-minute discussion over lunch.

OF APOSTOLIC CLOUDS AND TAKING OVER THE WORLD

So what's our real hope in all of this? Do we really expect every member of Granger Community Church to be on a mission in the world? Do we really expect that if they will replicate the fractal core that they will begin to make significant inroads for the kingdom of God in every domain of society? Do we honestly expect our people to embed themselves into gyms, schools, workplaces, neighborhoods, and networks where they can be knights, Jedi, tightrope walkers, highway planners, gardeners, cowboys, and geeks? Yes, actually, we do. In fact, we're banking on it. This is our best attempt to live out Jesus' revolutionary plot to take over the world!

As we finish talking about this missional move, let's look once more at a picture of what apostolic movement really looks like (fig. 11.4). We believe it will require *both* formal and fractal leadership.

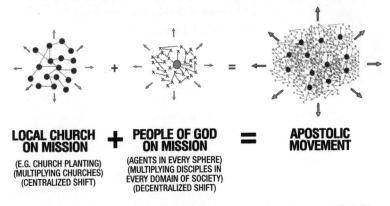

LOCAL CHURCH ON MISSION **+** **PEOPLE OF GOD ON MISSION** **=** **APOSTOLIC MOVEMENT**

(E.G. CHURCH PLANTING) (MULTIPLYING CHURCHES) (CENTRALIZED SHIFT)

(AGENTS IN EVERY SPHERE) (MULTIPLYING DISCIPLES IN EVERY DOMAIN OF SOCIETY) (DECENTRALIZED SHIFT)

Alan Hirsch and Dave Ferguson, *On the Verge* (Grand Rapids, Mich.: Zondervan, 2011), 74, adapted with permission.

Figure 11.4

When a local church is on mission, it will be able to leverage many of the things that no one of its individuals could hope to accomplish. Formal leadership is required to do this. We can take on the total transformation of an urban neighborhood like Monroe Circle or help to resource an entire church-planting movement in southern India. A local church can mobilize hundreds and thousands into significant points of focus and impact. A local church on mission is a beautiful thing, but it's not the complete picture. When a local church on mission also equips the people of God to internalize the fractal core and then releases them on mission into environments where the local church as a whole cannot or will not be able to go, then you have the makings of a movement! The local church gathered on mission gives you corporate presence and collective impact. The people of God scattered on mission, with the same fractal core, is an unstoppable, adaptable, reproducing force. With formal and fractal leadership, we have the potential for a true apostolic movement. Such are the building waves of the reverse tsunami that can sweep over our communities and the world with the grace of God.

Chapter 12

FROM INSTITUTION TO MOVEMENT
Missional Move 12

Jesus is the founder of the world's largest movement, today almost two billion strong. The New Testament documents capture its birth, depicting a dynamic, white-hot movement. The church began as a ragtag band of nobodies and over the course of three centuries became an unstoppable, world-transforming movement that threatened the world's rulers and their claims to power. According to Rodney Stark, an expert on the early church, what started as a small band in AD 30 had exploded by AD 350 into a viral, grassroots, decentralized network of thirty-three million people. At that time, Roman Emperor Constantine embraced Christianity and issued an edict of toleration. In truth, the edict was a long overdue recognition that the church had already won the empire by winning over the culture.

Since those early years, the church has continued to grow and change. St. Patrick led an innovative mission to the barbarians on the outskirts of the Roman Empire. John Wesley began the Methodist movement that swept the world like wildfire. William Booth began the Salvation Army and unleashed an unprecedented movement of humanitarian aid to the poor. Over the centuries, the Christian church has given birth to smaller movements that have influenced culture and shaped the world we live in today.

Sadly, when most people hear the words *church* or *Christianity*, a dynamic movement is not the first thing that comes to mind. Most of us tend to picture the church as a concrete religious institution with formal structures, old buildings, and hierarchical rules of order, rituals, and liturgy. Perhaps that is why people are sometimes attracted to Jesus, but not the church. Everyone longs to be a part of a movement, but virtually no one is fired up about assimilation into a religious institution.

Movements are catalytic, transformative, organic, relational, and exciting, conjuring up images of revolutions and revivals. So how does the church reclaim its primal identity as a movement?

A WORD ABOUT MOVEMENTS

As we have watched church planting reach movement status in India, we've seen firsthand the power of the church when it operates as an organic movement. Yet while we're grateful for what is happening in India, we aren't content to limit the "movemental" power of Christianity to other countries and cultural contexts. As leaders in the American church, we feel a longing for our own church, an ache that asks: "Why not here? Why not now? Why not us?" We have begun to sense that the American church is on the verge of something wonderful. But we also sense that for the church in the US to become a movement once again, it will require a new language, a new way of thinking about the church—much of which is still foreign to us in the West. So like anyone seeking to understand a new language, we've recognized a need to find someone who could speak "church-as-movement-ese" and translate it to those of us who speak "church-as-institution-ese."

A few summers back, when we (Rob and Michelle) took our

entire family to India for the first time, we planned a two-day layover in London to help break up the lengthy and grueling trip for our girls. While there, we had the joy of visiting the world-renowned British Museum, one of the largest gatherings of priceless historic artifacts from every continent and almost every area of human civilization. During our tour, I experienced a moment of deep wonder as we stood in front of the Rosetta Stone exhibit. This ancient stone was the key to unlocking the voice of ancient Egyptian culture, which had been "unhearable" for centuries prior. The Rosetta Stone has two different languages (Egyptian and Greek) inscribed upon it in three different scripts: hieroglyphic, demotic, and Greek. The overlapping of these languages and scripts released four thousand years of ancient written culture, making it understandable to us today. Before the Rosetta Stone was discovered, no one was able to decipher hieroglyphics. Now the stone is iconic, representative of any attempt to understand and "unlock" the hidden language of another culture.

In our attempts to "unlock" the culture of the church as a movement and translate it into the language of the institutional church, we discovered a "Rosetta Stone" that has proven immensely helpful. That Rosetta Stone was a book titled *The Forgotten Ways* by Alan Hirsch.[1] In *The Forgotten Ways*, Hirsch compellingly argues that all of God's people have everything within them needed to rediscover the church as a movement. Hirsch suggests that we think of this as a latent or dormant potential that needs to be discovered again and then activated. That's why throughout church history, and even today, it is possible to find examples of the church as a movement. The possibility of apostolic movement is always there, resident within each of us, waiting to be activated and unleashed. When we see a glimpse of it or read the stories about the church as a movement, something inside of us cries out, "That's it! That's where I belong!"

In his book, Hirsch introduces six elements, called mDNA, missional DNA, that are the genetic coding of the church as apostolic movement—the church we see in the pages of the New Testament, in past revivals, and currently in places like China and India. The mDNA are paradigmatic, defining a complete reformation of the form and function of the church. These six interrelated elements of mDNA provide the clearest snapshot of what it looks like to be a church as movement that we've yet encountered.[2]

Six Elements of mDNA[3]

1. *Jesus Is Lord.* The heart of any apostolic movement is the commitment to take Jesus and his claim to be Lord seriously.
2. *Disciple Making.* Apostolic movements occur when Jesus lives his life through us. We are apprenticed to Jesus.
3. *Missional-Incarnational Impulse.* This is the way in which the church engages culture by following God on his mission to the world.
4. *Apostolic Environment.* The ministry of the church is expressed in five forms that allow for growth and maturity.
5. *Organic Systems.* Apostolic movements are decentralized, but they are organized. Ministry is reconfigured so it is reproductive, fluid, and adaptive.
6. *Communitas.* Apostolic movements form a new kind of community life, one that thrives in the context of challenge, adventure, and risk.

To transition into a church that operates as a movement characterized by these six elements, we do not need to abandon the insights we have learned through the attractional and church-growth models of church. We simply need a more comprehensive paradigm that can include this thinking, but is not limited by it, a model that brings together the very best thinking and practices from different segments of the contemporary and historic expressions of the church. As Alan Hirsch and Dave Ferguson suggest in their book *On the Verge*, this new paradigm of the church as a movement is really "the result of the convergence of essentially three distinct ways of thinking about church — church-growth theory (which extends and maximizes traditional ecclesiology and organizes the church around the evangelistic function),"[4] exponential thinking (multiplication church planting), and incarnational missional approaches (reorienting the function and form of the church around the outward-bound function of mission and the inward-bound contextualization into every subculture). The goal, then, in becoming a movement-oriented church, is to integrate the best thinking and practices in megachurch with multisite and multiplication church planting with missional-incarnational approaches. In essence, we are seeking to recapture ancient truths while advancing into new expressions of the church for today.

Figure 12.1 is a diagram from *On the Verge* that provides a snapshot of the convergence that is happening.

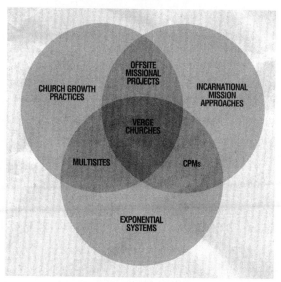

Alan Hirsch and Dave Ferguson, *On the Verge* (Grand Rapids, Mich.: Zondervan, 2011), 43, used with permission.

Figure 12.1

Churches that are seeking this convergence of the various approaches to mission are what Alan Hirsch and Dave Ferguson call *verge churches*. In *On the Verge*, they helpfully outline a three-step cycle that churches move through over and over again on the journey toward becoming an apostolic movement. They call this three-step process "movementum." Movementum is the process of gaining more and more "missional" momentum until a church births an apostolic movement. The three steps of the movementum process are (fig. 12.2):

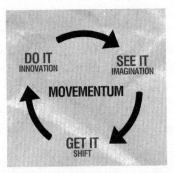

Alan Hirsch and Dave Ferguson, *On the Verge* (Grand Rapids, Mich.: Zondervan, 2011), 47, used with permission.

Figure 12.2

Step 1: See it. This first step involves what Hirsch and Ferguson call *missional imagination*—the ability to see the mission and the church as Jesus sees it.

Step 2: Get it. Next, we need to shift from seeing to *understanding* mission and church as Jesus does. This involves reshaping our vision and values.

Step 3: Do it. Finally, we must *do mission* and be the church in the way of Jesus. This leads to a reformation in our methodology, where the church corporately and the people of God individually believe and behave as the sent ones.

Hirsch and Ferguson envision the movementum process as an ongoing cycle, much like a flywheel that spins faster and faster with each turn of the wheel. To better understand what all of this looks like in the context of a local church, let's look at how that wheel began spinning at Granger and where we are today.

Further Reading

We hope, after reading this chapter, that you'll move beyond this book to the source material that underlies this shift. We recognize that as a church, we are just getting out of the gate, so we would encourage you to check out some of these "must reads" for more on this missional move:

- *The Forgotten Ways* by Alan Hirsch
- *On the Verge* by Alan Hirsch and Dave Ferguson
- *Movements That Change the World* by Steve Addison
- *Church 3.0* by Neil Cole
- *The Tangible Kingdom* and the *Tangible Kingdom Primer* by Hugh Halter
- *AND: The Gathered and Scattered Church* by Hugh Halter and Matt Smay

CHURCH AS MOVEMENT: SEE IT!

If the first step to gaining missional "movementum" is to "see it," how did we, at Granger, first begin to see? For almost twenty-four years, our attendance was growing, often with double-digit percentage increases. Then, around 2007, we stopped growing, and it nearly killed us. None of us were wired for maintenance. And we were determined—no matter what it took—to seek the face of God and find our way forward. Simply holding ground was not an option for us.

During that same season, something else was happening in both our local and global work as a church that soon became like a "splinter in our mind." We felt stuck in our Jerusalem, but our work in Judea, Samaria, and the ends of the earth was exploding. We began to see church differently as we lived on mission "out there"—both locally and globally. Soon, what we were seeing "out there" began to radically impact our understanding of church "back here."

At the local level, a decentralized, grassroots, micromovement emerged in a low-income housing project called Monroe Circle. This was a new area of growth for us, what Hirsch and Ferguson would label an *incarnational mission* approach. Monroe Circle Community Center became a learning lab as we began to resource and relate to the leaders and teams in the mission incarnational circle and create more decentralized and organic structures. We also rebooted our training based on questions like:

- How can we take a certain set of DNA—an irreducible minimum—and a few best practices—that are highly portable—and give people as much freedom as possible to adapt and contextualize that into their setting?
- How do we push the power and authority as far out as we can to the grassroots level?
- How do we avoid falling into the traditional template of church at Monroe Circle?
- How do we plant the Saved Wholes Gospel among these people and then let a culturally expressive, mission-driven, Jesus-centered, kingdom-focused church grow up out of it?

While all of this was happening, our work in India was ushering us into another paradigmatic understanding of the church—*exponential thinking*. Over the years, as we engaged in coaching church planters and pastors in India, we had been operating with an addition model of "growth." However, during the last few years of our work, we had begun crossing over into the world of "multiplication." We noticed the changes began when the message, "Every believer is a church planter; every church is a church-planting church," began to become a reality. Within twelve to eighteen months, each new church plant of twenty to fifty people was already identifying others within their group who were ready to begin the bore-well coaching process. These individuals would head out with the same missional DNA into a new pocket of unreached people. Within twenty-four months, each church had become a reproducing church, planting reproducing churches. Once this became the new normal, we had transitioned to multiplication—the basis for a vibrant movement. In one six-month window alone, more than 250 churches were planted!

These little platoons of churches typically don't have buildings. They meet in homes, under banyan trees, and in public spaces—one of them meets on the roof of a restaurant where the pastor works. These churches don't have professional, paid clergy. We've lowered the bar in how we define a church, while raising the bar on leadership development and discipleship. Instead of professionals, we recruit ordinary revolutionaries to lead these simple churches. But these aren't just small groups; they are fully functional churches—worshiping together, serving together, studying together, and leading others to Jesus together.

In both of these contexts, Monroe Circle and India, we were beginning to learn what it meant to be a movement church. We began to dream about what might happen if we would pull together these three circles—the best of the attractional church growth practices, the insights of incarnational missional approaches, and the thinking behind exponential multiplication—and let all three of them define us as a church. We had tasted the fruit from each of these movement models, and now we were wondering how to plant these hybrid seeds among our own people. We had "seen it" in various contexts; now we wanted to help our people "get it."

CHURCH AS MOVEMENT: GET IT!

Our experience in each of these contexts led us to develop a new vision statement, beginning with these words: "The differences at Granger Community Church in the next five years will be greater than the changes of the past twenty-five. Granger is not just an institution or location; we are a movement of people who understand we are Jesus' plan to transform and heal communities." Though we had always been a church that values innovation and change, with this new vision, we were preparing ourselves for a fresh season of changes. Now we were asking our people to change from the kinds of changes we'd made for the past twenty-five years. All of the changes we had made, to this point, were changes within the paradigm of the attractional church, changes based on church-growth strategies. Now we were hoping to move beyond that single paradigm into a whole new category of change—becoming an apostolic movement.

In the past, the leadership of the church simply sought God to determine the best next course of action, combined that vision with the expertise and wise counsel of godly people in leadership, and then steered the ship onto a course that followed that vision. This process was different.

Starting January 2010, we invited the people of Granger into an open-source process to reorient our vision around the idea of missional imagination and the church as apostolic movement. We began to gather input from as many people as we could—from our congregation and the community at large—to discover new ideas, unearth synergy, and create ownership for the vision to launch our next season of ministry. We brainstormed, listened, whiteboarded, texted, and surveyed, even creating an online portal where we gathered thousands of dreams for how our community could be different if the church was unleashed on God's mission. After every idea was considered, we compiled them to create a first draft of our vision and mission based on the areas of synergy we discovered. We discovered three themes that would eventually be summarized by the word BAR. We called the new vision "Raising the BAR," and it consisted of three elements:

1. Be the church.
2. Activate the campus.
3. Reproduce at every level.

The first draft of the vision statement was circulated via focus groups to hundreds of people within the core of our church. We asked them, "Is this closer to what you think Jesus is calling our church to be?" Again, every single piece of feedback was prayerfully considered. A second revision was developed and cycled for feedback. Ultimately, the statement went through five revisions and cycles of feedback. This exhaustive process involved thousands of people. It also provided us with countless opportunities to affirm our belief that every believer carries within them the potential for world transformation. The pastors weren't just telling the people, "Hey, we're the professionals. Here's the new vision." We were essentially asking them to tell us what God had laid on their hearts. We were saying to them, "Based on what we know in the book of Acts and what is resident inside of us through the Holy Spirit, what should our church look like five years from now?" You could almost see the missional impulse of the Holy Spirit awakening in the hearts of our people. Passion was ignited. Dangerous dreams were unleashed. This entire process ended up changing the very understanding of what church is for many of our people.

I remember one of the focus groups I led during this process. Though the meeting had officially ended, most of the people in this group of thirty remained to talk and continue the discussion. In fact, we were still going strong two hours past the end of the meeting! People shared things like, "I feel God has prepared me my whole life for this very moment," and, "Whatever it takes, whatever it costs, I'm in." Three hours after the meeting was over, our hosts had to graciously kick several people out of their house. That's a good problem to have.

> Interested in learning more on the process of vision development at Granger? Head to *missionalmoves.com* and look for a link to the ebook *Vision: Lost and Found* by our executive pastor, Tim Stevens.

Needless to say, the entire process created a groundswell of grassroots ownership. By the time we were prepared to roll out our new vision as a church, thousands of people had been deeply involved in the process. Their fingerprints were all over the vision statement. One young leader said to me, "It's easy to own the vision when you've been involved every step of the way. I know we have to officially roll this out for the weekend crowd, but I'm so far beyond that already. I decided I was all in months ago. Enough talk, let's do this!" I heard that same statement reflected over and over again in the comments people shared with me. When we rolled out the new vision, it was met with a standing ovation. We had changed the story of our church. There was now a new paradigm operating at the core. It felt, to many of us, as if one chapter of our history had ended and another begun (fig. 12.3). This rebirth of our vision and values—and especially the process by which it was birthed—gave our church a feeling of being planted afresh, of starting over once again. That's the dynamic of an apostolic movement.

A CASE OF CONTRASTS

These are some of the ways we're thinking about the differences in the new vision.

CHAPTER 1 (1986-2010)	CHAPTER 2 (2011 and beyond)
Get the community into the church.	Get the church into the community.
Church planting focus in India.	Church planting focus worldwide.
Church defined largely by weekend service.	Church defined by "where you are."
Primarily centralized, top-down structure.	Primarily decentralized and organic movement.
Primary stats are attendance and giving.	We begin also tracking community impact and "loving others."
Buildings serve the church—the community is invited to join.	Buildings serve the community—the congregation also meets there.
One central campus, two other gathering places.	Hundreds of gathering places.
Everything branded "Granger Community Church."	"Granger Community Church" is The HUB of a larger movement.
People come to the church building to do their ministry.	Ministry isn't confined to a building. It happens wherever you are.
Separate ministry for children, youth and adults.	A comprehensive family ministry that encompasses the entire spiritual development of the child and education of the parents.
Want to get married? Need a place for a funeral? Find another building.	We will have dedicated staff and space to stand with you and support you on these days of transition or crisis.

Figure 12.3

We also began developing an education plan to move our entire community deeper into the new paradigm of an apostolic movement. We took our executive staff through both the *Forgotten Ways* and the *Forgotten Ways* video series. We mapped an education plan for the entire staff, creating a curriculum with video resources that could be used in different settings. And we changed the focus of our annual conference to talk about the genius of the *And* approach, incorporating the best insights of the attractional and missional models together (*andconference.com*).

In addition, we are developing weekend series around the idea of church as movement. For example, we built a series around the idea of "missional impulse" called cow-tipping. The idea is that it's time to tip our sacred cows, those institutionally bound definitions of church that we are afraid to change. We've also intentionally elevated the stories of people who are engaged in missional living where God has placed them, sharing stories of transformation taking place in diverse places—from public schools to yoga studios.

Finally, we joined the Future Travelers (*missional.com*), a cohort of pioneering leaders who've been successful at the prevailing megachurch/multisite model of church and are now asking serious questions about the future. Each of these churches is piloting more missional and incarnational expressions of church via their megachurches. By the end of this two-year process, we had a profound sense that our people could not only see the new vision (missional imagination); they were starting to understand it as well. We had moved from "see it" to "get it," and were ready to do something about it.

CHURCH AS MOVEMENT: DO IT!

During a trip to Rome, our founding pastor, Mark Beeson, was visiting a large, famous church to take some pictures. He entered the church building and noticed that a worship service was underway. *Should I interrupt?* he wondered. And then he noticed something

Mark Beeson

Santa Maria Maggiore

odd. All over the basilica were tourists just like him, roaming around and looking at the architecture and taking pictures, while the small group of congregants sat and listened to the service. Mark comments on his experience and how it spoke to him of the challenges facing the church in the West:

"It felt a little odd. But setting my little mini-tripod at the back of the church facing straight up the center aisle—during the service—was actually the least-intrusive behavior I observed. I think I counted more tourists roaming around the great basilica than congregants seated for worship.

"Seeing the hordes of tourists in that church made me wonder if the church in the West isn't far from the scene I witnessed in Rome. Church sociologists tell us that 40 percent of the population can be reached with our current ministry strategies. If so, that's fantastic—for the 40 percent. But that means 60 percent of the population may need further interpretation and a better translation of the gospel.

"Like tourists swinging through on their way to check out the Coliseum and the Trevi Fountain, people visit our churches or see what we are doing and think, 'That's nice for you, but it's just not for me.' They see what we're doing, but what we're doing isn't impacting them enough to transform their lives with God's love. They're unfazed and untouched. So they snap a few photos and move along, hoping their tour through life will eventually show them something more captivating and more engaging.

"We're working on ways we can better translate the gospel for the 60 percent while serving well the 40 percent. I think the task is most worthwhile."

Churches all over Europe that were once vibrant hubs for kingdom transformation are now tourist spots marked for Kodak moments. Many of them have more tourists snapping photos on a Sunday morning than people gathered to worship the risen Lord. These places were once the megachurches of their day. Now they are nothing but museums.

Is that our future? Here at Granger we've decided, "Not if we have anything to do with it!"

The final three missional moves we have left to unpack will show how we at Granger are moving forward, putting our missional imagination to work through innovation.

Chapter 13

FROM MEGA AND MULTI TO MEGA, MULTI, AND MICRO
Missional Move 13

Many of us can feel it in our bones, a holy discontent—a splinter in the mind—that tells us that things are changing. As Mark Beeson would say, "The church is not a field to be fenced, but a force to be unleashed." As we have shared, we have seen God do some truly amazing things through the prevailing models of church growth. According to Dave Olson's research in *Crisis in the American Church*, mega- and multisite churches are the only groups of churches categorically growing over the past thirty years. But among the leaders of these prevailing models there are nagging questions, like:

- What if we really believed that every member of our church is a missionary?
- What if the seed for world transformation really is planted in the heart of every single follower of Jesus?
- If the primal identity of church is a bottom-up, grassroots movement, what does that mean in terms of our everyday life as a congregation?

These questions leave us searching hard for what God has next, not the next greatest program, series idea, or fad. We're searching for an innovation that goes down to the very core of what it means to be the church. What if the longing and discontent stirring inside the leading practitioners of successful mega- and multisite churches are signs of the next great move of God, one of historic proportions?

As we addressed earlier, there has been a growing divide in the church now between those advocating a missional model of mission engagement and those advocating a more attractional model. But as we suggested in the last chapter, a growing number of practitioners from within both the attractional and the missional camp are now seeing a possibility that only exists in combining the best of both models. Alan Hirsch and Dave Ferguson make this interesting observation: "It is only those who have really mastered the prevailing paradigm that are most often the first ones to break with the consensus—e.g., Einstein and Heisenberg in science, or Luther and Calvin in theology—real experts are the only ones most able and likely to perceive when things are wrong!"[1] Thomas Kuhn, in his book *The Structure of Scientific Revolutions*, describes this as the "roaming of the mind."[2] As they reflect on their current paradigm, a "splinter in the mind" develops, an anomaly, and along with it a growing sense of something being wrong. This turns into conversation with others who experience the same discontent, which in turn leads to new initiatives and experiments led by these dissenters, and eventually a new paradigm develops. What if we are at that moment?

That brings us to the next missional move, the shift from mega and multi to mega, multi, and micro. We believe the time has come to move beyond our current fascination with megachurches and multisite models to a broader focus on microchurch movements.

For decades, churches in the West have perfected the megachurch model, and over the past decade many churches have embraced the path to multisite, but as helpful as these approaches are, we believe that a further step is needed at the micro level.

What is the microchurch level? *Micro* describes the type of church where every member lives as a missionary. Micro is another way of referring to a church that intentionally plants a missional community among every subculture in a community. In a microchurch, ordinary men and woman are equipped to plant their own simple church in their workplace or neighborhood. Every member is equipped and released to unleash their ministry, not as a volunteer at the campus, but as a way of life in the domain of society where God has already placed them.

Todd Wilson, leader of the Exponential Network, asks, "What if God has uniquely positioned the prevailing Mega/Multi church as the distribution system for the Micro? Contrary to what many would like to see (the deconstruction or bashing of the prevailing MEGA/MULTI), what if we are to celebrate and catalyze its incredible capacity to propel Micro forward in a more viral way than we've ever seen ...?"[3]

We are on a journey with a learning cohort comprised of twelve megachurches representing more than eighty thousand people who are seeking to answer Todd's question. The lifecycle for apostolic movements in the West is only in the embryonic stage. Therefore, what you'll see in this chapter, and the coming chapters, is not a well-oiled machine, but a work in progress. We're just out of the starting blocks. We feel so raw, we weren't even sure about including these last five missional moves! So why did we include them? Trusted mentors and church leaders in the trenches repeatedly encouraged us, saying, "Don't wait. We actually need to see the work in progress, instead of just a 'finished product.' We need to see the process."

Attractional thinking about the church offers a clearly defined model that can be replicated. Missional thinking, on the other hand, doesn't have a standardized model. Missional requires many models, since each model of cultural engagement must be developed and contextualized for every unique setting. Our goal, then, is not to show you a model for becoming a missional church but to give you the process for how we got there. This begins by looking at how we've been able to leverage our strengths as a multisite megachurch to serve as the launching pad for a microchurch movement. To do this, we will begin with a few nonnegotiable micro maxims. These are the fundamental beliefs required for a microchurch movement to become viable.

MICRO MAXIM 1: REPRODUCTION IS GOD'S DESIGN FOR EVERYONE

A while back Rick Warren asked a group of seasoned leaders, "What is a mature church?" Mark Beeson, our pastor at Granger, immediately knew his response: "The 'mature church' is the church filled with immaturity. Anywhere in the world, whether plant or animal, the clear delineation of 'maturity' is the ability to reproduce. Immature animals can't reproduce. Immature plants can't replicate themselves. The definition of maturity is 'being fully ripe, fully aged,' so the connotation of maturity is obvious. Where you see maturity you'll observe new life, babies, and immaturity all over the place. Maturity desires reproduction."[4] Mature churches are filled with immaturity because they are reproducing churches. The truest sign of maturity is ongoing reproduction in the life of a church and in the lives of individual believers.

In Genesis, we read God's command at the conclusion of the creation narrative, "Be fruitful and multiply. Fill the earth."[5] In other words, God's first command was, "Reproduce!" Because of humanity's failure to obey and keep that command, God entered the creation to recreate this world and restore shalom. The plan for restoration, however, continued the original mandate of reproduction. Just as he commanded human beings in the garden to be fruitful and reproduce, Jesus now gives that command to the church through the mandate of the Great Commission—make disciples and reproduce! In the first creation narrative, our call from God was to make babies and fill the earth with the fruit of human creativity, stewarding the material resources God had given to us. Now, in the new creation narrative, our call is to make disciples and fill the earth with followers of Jesus, people who represent God's perfect image. In both narratives, the outcome is the same: reproduction. Every follower of Jesus should be a reproducing follower of Jesus. And every church should be a reproducing church. If we believe that reproduction is God's will for all of us, then we will build our systems accordingly. But if we believe that reproduction is a rare character trait, only for the exceptional, then we will build our systems accordingly.

Virtually all the systems the church has developed over the last seventeen hundred years have been designed for a single local church where there is one person (the pastor) who takes the responsibility for reproduction. What does the structure and programming of your church reveal about your own view of reproduction? When you truly believe that reproduction is the call of every believer, you'll find yourself dreaming about creating systems that develop that inherent reproductive ability in every follower of Jesus.

MICRO MAXIM 2: MULTIPLICATION IS GOD'S PLAN FOR EVERYONE

Reproduction and multiplication go hand in hand. As every follower of Jesus becomes a reproducing follower of Jesus, we move from models of growth based on addition to models based on multiplication. God's design for his people is multiplication. Robert Coleman, author of the *Master Plan of Evangelism*, emphasizes this when he writes, "The ultimate goal of Jesus for his disciples was that his life be reproduced in them and through them into the lives of others.... Reproduction was our Lord's desire ... but multiplication was the ultimate end."[6] In fact, throughout his ministry, Jesus taught and emphasized multiplication as the norm for his followers. He did this using various metaphors, including:

- *Fruit (John 15).* Fruit bearing is referred to more than fifty times in the New Testament. In John 15:2–8, Jesus reiterates that fruit will multiply in the lives of his disciples. He told them to expect not only "fruit" (v. 2), but "more fruit (v. 5), and even "much fruit" (v. 8). Ultimately, Jesus says it is "much fruit" and the multiplication of fruit that glorifies the Father.

- *Talents (Matthew 25).* The two-talent servant through his faithfulness multiplied the two into four. The five-talent servant multiplied his five to ten. Both of these multipliers were told, "Well done, good and faithful servant!" (vv. 21, 23). Faithfulness leads to fruitfulness, which leads to multiplication.

- *Seed (Mark 4).* With the seed, we are promised that multiplication is the expected outcome: "Still other seed fell on good soil. It came up, grew and produced a crop, some multiplying thirty, some sixty, some a hundred times" (v. 8). When the seed hits that good soil, it multiplies and spreads. To drive home the point, Mark stacks a couple more multiplication stories on top of the parable of the sower, including the parable of the growing seed and the parable of the mustard seed, with the outcome of multiplication being the smallest seed producing the "largest of all" (v. 32).

- *Yeast, Dough, and Bread (Matthew 13–15).* Once the yeast is in the dough and the heat in the oven is cranked up, multiplication happens. Adding a surprising twist, the amount of dough the woman in this passage is working with is ridiculously large. But it's nothing the power of multiplication can't handle. Those little pockets of CO_2 will multiply and expand, lifting the entire loaf. Big problems can only be solved through multiplying small. We all know what happens when Jesus gets a few loaves in his hands; he multiplies them and makes them a meal for thousands.

The book of Acts carries on the theme of multiplication by telling the story of the early church, how the earliest followers of Jesus rapidly multiplied from Jerusalem to the farthest edges of the Roman Empire. Multiplication is recorded and emphasized in the record of the early church (Acts 1:15; 2:41; 4:4; 6:7; 9:31; 12:24;

16:5; 19:20; 28:30–31). So how do we, once again, recapture the power of multiplication that was at work in such powerful ways in the early church? Multiplication won't happen with our existing megachurch models, nor is multisite the hoped-for solution. While retaining the insights of both these approaches, we need the explosive, viral power of multiplication that a microchurch emphasis brings to the equation. Megachurches and multisite churches bring centralized resources and capacity to propel the microchurch (missional) movement forward in a more viral way than we've ever seen in North America. None of these movements will be able to reach their full potential without the other.

MICRO MAXIM 3: DISCIPLE MAKING HAPPENS BEST THROUGH MICRO

Jesus asked us to make disciples. After our personal commitment to the lordship of Jesus, nothing matters more than disciple making. Everything rises and falls on our ability as a local church to make disciples. In the older church-growth model, the weekend service was the catalytic engine that was designed to power everything else. But in apostolic movement, while the weekend service has an important role, disciple making is seen as that catalytic engine. Microenvironments are naturally conducive settings for transformation. Why? Because microenvironments are simply life-on-life relationships between people that grow and develop in the context of shared mission, rather than organized programs. Microchurch thinking emphasizes that disciple making is a team sport, something that best happens in small to midsized teams (ten to twenty people) with smaller gatherings of two to three people within those teams. This is how Jesus did his own discipleship. He had a large group of seventy-two, a smaller team of twelve, and an inner circle of three. The early church met in homes, subdivided into smaller groups, and you'll find a similar pattern in past movements like Methodism (societies, bands, and classes) or modern movements like the house church in China. Although mega- and multi-church environments have created incredible momentum for growth through corporate shepherding, microenvironments are the best settings for engaging in personal shepherding—the transformation that happens through one-on-one relationships.

Corporate Shepherding	Personal Shepherding
focuses on the macro	focuses on the micro
focuses on the masses	focuses on the individual
focuses on standardization	focuses on customization
focuses on programs to accomplish goals	focuses on processes to transform people
focuses on centralized processes	focuses on decentralized processes
focuses on normalization	focuses on adaptability/ incarnation

At first glance, this comparison might seem to villainize the corporate shepherding process. Again, though, rather than thinking of these as a pure contrast, think of the differences as places on a continuum. The key is finding ways to integrate the best of both approaches. We see this in the wonderful pattern in Acts, where the early church gathered together as a large group in the temple courts and also met house to house. Both are important. Corporate shepherding without personal shepherding leaves people feeling like "sheep without a shepherd." Simultaneously, personal shepherding can be dramatically enhanced when it is done in the context of dynamic corporate shepherding. Through corporate shepherding, we create environments, much like a greenhouse, where thousands of individuals are helped to grow in their relationship with Christ. Still, many mega- and multi-site church leaders are now reaching a "halftime" moment, having invested two or three decades of their life into the prevailing model, and are deeply unsettled by some of the unintended outcomes of the prevailing models. The Willow Creek Association's REVEAL study[7] confirmed the nagging questions regarding our program-based, building-centric approach to discipleship, helping many church leaders better understand that the primary pathway to discipleship is not in a church building or a Sunday service but in life-to-life discipleship that happens "out there" on mission in the world.

Many church leaders still believe that most spiritual formation is likely to happen at a service or in a class at church. By contrast, micro thinking embraces the uncomfortable reality that most spiritual formation must and often can happen only at home and at work, outside the programs and scheduled times when people meet for church activities. As we mentioned in Missional Move 5 ("From the Center to the Margins"), the poor, the lost, and the marginalized aren't likely to attend our churches, so only when believers are out on mission in the world are they being formed and transformed by their engagement with the poor. As church leaders, we will give an account not for the health of our programs but for the health of our people. We can no longer simply measure our success by the quality and attendance of our programs. Microchurch thinking measures success by the quality of people—how well are we molding and shaping them into wholehearted disciples of Jesus?

MICRO MAXIM 4: SMALL AND SIMPLE REPRODUCES BETTER THAN LARGE AND COMPLEX

Mark Beeson has often reminded us, "The more complex something is, the more it can do, but the easier it is to break. The simpler something is, the less it can do, but the harder it is to break." The same is true with reproduction in biological systems. Small and simple organisms reproduce better than large and complex organisms. Microenvironments reproduce better and faster than larger ones.

Consider this thought experiment from the brilliant book *The Rabbit and the Elephant: Why Small Is the New Big for Today's*

Church.[8] Imagine you take Mama Elephant and Papa Elephant, provide the perfect romantic setting, and set the mood. Turn up a little Marvin Gaye and make sure there are plenty of peanuts. Turn down the lights and let magic happen. Return two years later and what do you have? Mom, Dad, and baby make three. The gestation process for elephants is twenty-two long months (think of *that*, ladies!).

Before

After

Rabbits come at the task of reproduction a totally different way. They don't need Marvin Gaye to get into the mood. If anything, rabbits, like other rodents, seem to need very little to drive their sexual urges.

Rabbits get right down to business. Gestation for a rabbit is thirty days. At the end of the two years, when you knock on the door to check on Mama and Papa Rabbit, you will find yourself negotiating a tide of fur and cottontails as you struggle to outrun the surge. In fact, at a point in the not-too-distant future, your ability to kill the creatures individually is outstripped by their ability to reproduce.

Before

After

This is indeed how the early church grew, and it wasn't until Constantine's legalization of Christianity in the fourth century that the rabbit movement began to grow a trunk and start weighing pounds and tons rather than ounces at a time.

The Dales and Barna conclude, "A megachurch is like an elephant. It is easily visible and dominates the landscape. A major effort of both money and manpower is required to produce another megachurch."[9] The same is true of multisite. Both mega and multi environments are big and complex in terms of leadership, management, infrastructure, services, resources, and facilities. Large and complex is hard to reproduce. By contrast, however, small and simple can reproduce quickly and easily: "A microchurch (simple church, organic church, house church, or *missional community*) is like a rabbit. Rabbits live underground and you cannot easily find them, but they are everywhere ... they have the potential for rapid multiplication because ... they are very easy to duplicate. A plague of 'rabbit' churches could transform a nation."[10]

> Check out Mark Beeson's thoughts on "Dinosaurs, Mice, and 250 Tons of Biomass" at *missionalmoves.com*.

MISSIONAL COMMUNITIES AND ESSENTIAL CHURCHES

When we talk about micro expressions of the church, we are referring to what some have called missional communities. Hugh Halter, the director of Missio and author of *Tangible Kingdom*, defines missional communities as "intentional webs of relationships bound together for the express purpose of bringing to light the kingdom of God to those outside the faith."[11] Jeff Vanderstelt, the lead pastor of Soma Communities, defines a missional community as a "family of missionary servants who make disciples who make disciples."[12] And Mike Breen, the leader of 3DM and former pastor of St. Thomas Sheffield Church, explains that a missional community is "a group of twenty to fifty people who exist, in Christian community, to reach either a particular neighborhood or network of relationships. With a strong value on life together, the group has the expressed intention of seeing those they are in relationship with choose to start following Jesus through this more flexible and locally incarnated expression of the church. They exist to bring heaven to the particular slice of earth they believe God has given them to bless. The result is usually the growth and multiplication of more Missional Communities."[13]

Here's how we have defined a missional community at Granger: "A missional community is a reproducing group of people living together on mission to *be* the church among an unreached pocket of people."

Most of these missional communities will be around twenty to fifty people, a smaller "church" within the larger corporate church. They are comprised of people committed to living outward beyond themselves and to demonstrating the gospel in word and deed in their neighborhood, workplace, or the specific pocket of people they are called to reach and serve. Missional communities serve among the 40 percent who have some limited contact with the church (fig. 13.1). They do this by integrating their life into the life of the community being served at one of our ministry sites or through the Monroe Circle Community Center.

THE SHRINKING 40%

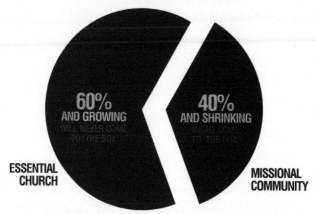

Figure 13.1

Our missional communities are effective at connecting people in our church with specific communities where we have an established presence. But what about the people who will never darken the door of a church? What about those who have little to no contact with the church? Since the people we are trying to reach in these communities won't come to church, we will take the church to them. We call these missional communities *essential churches*. Functionally, essential churches are exactly the same as our missional communities—with one exception. They intentionally target folks in the "growing 60 percent" who are not in close enough cultural proximity to be reached by our current expressions at our sites. In fact, in most cases any attempt to integrate regularly with a site would actually hinder the establishment of the church within the subculture they are called to reach. Essential churches have the flexibility to create culturally incarnated expressions of church for the unreached pocket of people they live among.

What you decide to call your essential church is not all that important. Essential church leaders don't walk around saying, "Hey, we're an essential church. Want to join?" We refer to these communities as essential churches because they represent the lowering of the bar, a return to the essentials of what constitutes a Christian church. Our strategy is simple: keep it small and allow it to reproduce. Some of these essential churches will develop leaders who will eventually pursue a more traditional church-planting approach, so these communities also function as something of a farm system for additional leaders and planters.

But what, exactly, characterizes a missional community or an essential church? In concrete terms, we look for a group of twenty to fifty people that

- is centered on living out the lordship of Jesus together.
- exists to make disciples.

So ... What Does It Actually Look Like?

Jason, at the ripe old age of thirty-one, is an "elder" in the skating "tribe" gathered in a small town just north of Granger's main campus. Jason's mad skills on a board and a bike have given him the respect of this clan. But it's much more than that. This clan is composed mostly of teenagers and twentysomethings from broken families who live on the edges. Jason, although he is one of them, is a curiosity because he is not only a skater but also a happily married husband and a deeply engaged father. Most of this tribe has never seen that before, not among one of their members. Together, along with a few friends, one of which owns a skate shop, they are planting the gospel through word and deed.

Recently, Jason invited the tribe to have a deeper look into his life. Each day, he created a short video with his cell phone that he uploaded to YouTube so his tribe could see "what my everyday life with Jesus is like." One day, he's out skating at the park, he wipes out, and lands ... on his head! The next day, he's playing with his little boy and they make up a rap. One video features him washing the dishes for his wife. Jason is very transparent and direct about his faith and clearly shares how grace touches every area of life, but he's not preachy. A few of the videos have a strong artistic flair, featuring Jason rapping or creating graffiti. (In his basement, by the way. No laws were broken!) I have to admit, half the time I can't fully understand what Jason is even saying. Why? Because the good news is being expressed through the culture of that tribe, of which I am not a member. Put me on a board and I'll end up in a hospital. But like a good missionary, Jason speaks their language fluently. Each video is embedded with the symbols, dialect, and metaphor of that tribe. Each day, you can see the videos have each been viewed somewhere between forty to fifty times, which is the size of that tribe. That means virtually every member of his tribe is on the journey into the gospel with Jason. He is already discipling them before they are even converted. He's sharing with them a life in the way of Jesus.

- shares a common mission of proclaiming the gospel among their pocket of people through a mixture of verbal proclamation (Word) and demonstration proclamation (strategic service).
- lives among the pocket of people on a daily basis. That incarnational living is demonstrated through frequency, proximity, and spontaneity.
- looks for the "person of peace" in their community of desired impact. Jesus gave us a simple strategy for our mission. Look for the person who welcomes you, receives you, serves you, and responds to you. A person of peace is the gatekeeper to a whole network of relationships.
- meets formally on a regular basis in a "low-bar meeting" to engage the Scripture, encourage corporate practices, and deepen community.
- is led by laypeople, who receive ongoing coaching, training, and accountability.
- is made up of smaller groups of two or three people each (Life Transformation Groups) that provide peer-based pastoring and challenge toward mission and shared core practices.
- does not require people to be professing followers of Jesus to belong.
- is reproducing. The mindset from day one is "Our missional community will multiply."

The important thing to note in this description is that the traditionally held centralization of authority and the capacity to replicate and grow the church has been made "fractal." We've simplified it and placed it into the hands of men, women, families, and students who can more effectively and strategically reach those around them.

As you can see, we're not just after a stampede of rabbits. We are looking for diverse expressions of church, ways in which believers can be both scattered *and* gathered in one large movement. To visualize what we are after, consider what happens in a forest or a jungle during a fire. As the fire spreads, it's not just the rabbits that

So ... It's Like Small Groups, Right? Yeah, We've Already Got Those.

You might be wondering, "Aren't these microenvironments the same thing as small groups or small group Bible studies? Isn't this just a repackaging of stuff that most of us have been doing for years?" Great question. The answer is no. Microenvironments like the ones we're talking about are not just the latest reincarnation of small groups. Here is what most churches typically think of when they talk about small groups:

- Groups of five to ten people.
- People register through the organized church via a sign-up list or website portal.
- Individuals are placed into a group by a pastor or staff person.
- They show up once a week for a ninety-minute meeting that consists of eating snacks, drinking coffee, praying, and discussing the chapter in the book they didn't quite get to finish before the meeting.
- After the meeting is dismissed, everyone continues their mostly separate and disconnected lives.

Can a small group be more than this? Of course, and many are much more! Some small groups are experiencing the kind of vibrant, mission-centered community the early church experienced, but any quick survey of church leaders will tell you that most small groups tend toward the insular focus described in our list. Most small groups begin and end with the pursuit of community, with mission as a tag-on that becomes an occasional activity.

Over the last few years, Matt Carter, lead pastor of Austin Stone Community Church, has challenged the more than two hundred small groups in his congregation to change from small groups into missional communities. At the point of writing this book, about 30 percent of these groups have successfully made the transition. Matt sees some clear differences between traditional small groups and missional communities, but more than anything else, the difference is evident in the reason the group exists. Matt summarizes, "We discovered, if you aim for community as the goal, you don't get mission. If you aim for mission as the goal, you almost always get community."

Microenvironments like these missional communities and our essential churches begin, first and foremost, with mission and then build a community around that mission.

run. You'll find elephants, antelope, deer, lions, and almost anything else that can leap or fly. We believe God is lighting a fire in the church, and we are preparing for a stampede of every possible incarnation and expression of the kingdom of God in our midst. The rabbits will spread, but so will the elephants. Is your church ready to learn from both?

Chapter 14

FROM "WE CAN DO IT; YOU CAN HELP" TO "YOU CAN DO IT; WE CAN HELP"

Missional Move 14

The hope for the church in the West lies in the release of ordinary people on mission. The prevailing forms of church (contemporary church, multisite church, and megachurch) will never be effective at reaching all people. Alan Hirsch has spent considerable time considering several emerging trends in his home country of Australia. As you read his words, think about the trends in your own community—are there any similarities?

> In Australia, we have the somewhat farcical situation of 95 percent of evangelical churches tussling with each other to reach 12 percent of the population (those open and attracted to the prevailing models of church). And this becomes a significant missional problem because it raises the question, "What about the vast majority of the population (in Australia's case, 85 percent) that report alienation from *precisely* that form of church?" How do they assess the Gospel if they reject this form of church? And what would church be like for them in their various settings? Because what is

clear from the research in Australia, at least, is that when surveyed about what *they* think about the contemporary church growth expression of Christianity, the 85 percent range from being blasé ("good for them, but not for me") to total repulsion ("I would never go there"). At best, we can make inroads on the blasé; we can't hope to reach the rest of the population with this model—they are simply alienated from it and don't like it for a whole host of reasons.[1]

Like Hirsch, we celebrate what God has done and is doing through the prevailing models of church. But we also recognize the problem he raises: current expressions of the church are just not enough to take us into God's future. We'll need new forms—new ways of doing church—but what do these other forms of church look like?

What frightens the forces of darkness is not a swelling megachurch filled with people who rarely interact with the non-Christian world. Instead, the enemy fears a man who loves golf and plays with his friends from work, friends who would never come to church. This man and his wife serve these golf buddies, patiently entering their world, inviting them over for dinner, and watching their kids so they can have a date night. He encourages his buddies to participate in a golf tournament that benefits kids with disabilities. He develops the relationship, looking for natural opportunities to talk about his faith. And these relationships continue into the workplace, where golf games turn into lunches, cross-departmental collaboration, and rallying his own department's team to help a buddy hit his numbers for a bonus. Eventually, these relationships become vital friendships. That's what living incarnationally means. Again, Alan Hirsch writes, "When we talk of the Incarnation with a capital 'I,' we refer to that act of sublime love and humility whereby God takes it upon himself to enter into the depths of our world, our life, our reality in order that the redemption and consequent union between God and humanity may be brought about. This 'enfleshing' of God is so radical and total that it qualifies all subsequent acts of God in this world."[2]

Our engagement in mission will always embody itself incarnationally in the things we do every day. Mission is the *what*, while incarnation is the *how*. Combine these and you get something powerful, what Hirsch calls the *mission-incarnational impulse*: "The missional-incarnational impulse is, in effect, the practical outworking of the mission of God (the *missio Dei*) and of the Incarnation. It is thus rooted in the very way that God has redeemed the world, and in how God revealed himself to us."[3] A movement of ordinary Christ-followers living out their mission incarnationally in their everyday world can be a thousand times more powerful than a pastor speaking from a platform in a large church. Mission is not meant to be a category of activity that we try to fit into the discretionary time slot in our lives as a volunteer who serves on the weekend or a member who brings a friend to church. It is something that involves all of life. When volunteering or bringing a friend to church is the overflow of an incarnational lifestyle, it's beautiful. When it is a substitute for that, we've settled for a domesticated version of Christianity that will never change the world.

Ask yourself, "As a local church, where do we allocate our time, energy, and resources?" Most churches would have to admit that the vast majority of resources go toward equipping people to support the services and programs of the church, typically led by the staff. We affectionately call this approach, "We can do it; you can help."

But what if we structured for the opposite approach, one that says, "You can do it; we can help"? What if we spent our resources equipping people to realize that every Christ-follower has already been strategically placed in environments where they are poised to be the best conduit for the gospel? How do we unleash a movement of ordinary revolutionaries to live out their missional impulse incarnationally—all day, every day in the places where they live?

Here at Granger, the first part of answering that question has centered in a shift in the way we think about ourselves. This shift, then, began to change the way we equipped people to do the ministry

God was calling them to do. For starters, we began to realize there was a perception among some of our people that we were just trying to "get *them* to do *our* thing." Serve in our ministry, give to our cause, support our program, join our team, volunteer for our project, or come to our event. It's not that they didn't love our local church and its vision. They did; many of them had been among the most committed members of our church. After some time and prayer, we began to realize that it wasn't a matter of them not owning the vision of the church. Instead, God was awakening a missional impulse inside of them that required them to move toward something outside of our centralized efforts. This wasn't something to denigrate; it was something to celebrate! We also knew it would require yet another missional move on our part. To effectively equip and send people out, we needed to transform that restlessness into something productive while helping people feel valued, encouraged, equipped, and connected. We began by creating new expectations, new targets, and new tools.

NEW EXPECTATIONS

We started by changing both the language that we use to explain why we want people to participate and the expectation for what the final outcome will be. To use a military image, we reprogrammed our boot camp. In the military, boot camp is the foundational starting point for armed combat. Boot camp establishes norms for service, fitness, education, and a general set of skills necessary to be ready for battle. Once boot camp is finished, you deploy to active war zones. Boot camp is not the final destination; it's a foundation that prepares you for real-world scenarios where the skills you learn will be put to the test.

The Boot-Camp Model

We began by looking at the ministry infrastructure of Granger as a boot camp. To be clear, we aren't suggesting that our ministry teams at Granger aren't engaged on a daily basis in frontline, hand-to-hand combat. The boot-camp image, however, reminds us all that our goal is not to have people forever serving on an organized ministry team, as helpful and effective as they are. The goal of these teams is for people to be prepared for seasons in different fields of ministry. The boot-camp experience of a ministry team provides a place for a person to learn what works so they are better prepared to live out their missional impulse in another environment. It's entirely possible, for instance, that God is placing a desire in one of our members to reach the apartment complex where they live. So we invite them to come with us to Monroe Circle for a season where they learn some good practices for ministry before trying them out in their own setting. Once they graduate from boot camp, they can begin to build a team of like-minded Christ followers in their own neighborhood.

For a certain number of people, their God-given desires would integrate tightly with existing teams in our local church. That, too, is an exciting calling. In the military, those who stay in the boot-camp environment over time are called drill sergeants. Their role is clear and essential to the mission: they equip and reproduce more soldiers for the fight. Those who stay long-term on the in-house ministry teams are increasingly being asked to assume a similar role. Again, our goal is for every follower of Jesus to be a reproducing follower of Jesus.

The University Model

Our church is located in northern Indiana near the University of Notre Dame. If you live in this area, you will soon be astounded at the unbelievable loyalty of the alumni and students who attend Notre Dame. With each home football game, the community is flooded with millions of dollars and tens of thousands of alumni who return to watch their beloved Fighting Irish duke it out against ... well ... whomever. As many alumni will readily attest, one of the biggest advantages of a Notre Dame education is not just the education itself, but the international network of welcoming alumni who not only give generously to the university's endowment but hire Notre Dame graduates and take them under their wings to guarantee their success in the real world. In return, Notre Dame lavishly flaunts its well-to-do graduates and is notorious for priding itself on their success.

Notre Dame is seldom hurting for finances, and is successful at generating strong loyalty among its alumni, all while maintaining a network of far-reaching influence. In addition, the university has maintained a place in our community as a perennial powerhouse for employment, education, and influence. But how? By setting expectations and giving people a clear sense of identity. For example, success for a Notre Dame graduate is not getting their degree and then enrolling again for a new round of classes. Rather, the goal is graduating so that they can go out into the world and make something of themselves, remembering where they came from and who helped them to get there. Notre Dame gives its alumni a sense of shared identity as well. Each year, the school is able to take twelve thousand people from massively diverse experiences and give them a singular identity. Even people who just graduated find commonality with people who graduated fifty years ago. The university has a "Your glory is our glory" sort of perspective. Because of that, they spend a significant amount of time helping to network their graduates into a vast, diverse field of successful graduates. This engenders a feeling of intense loyalty among the graduates not only for their educational experience but also for the head start they received because of the network. Finally, Notre Dame provides its students with a hands-on experience. Notre Dame students are everywhere. The average Notre Dame student has the maximum opportunity to experience as many real-world environments pertinent to their educational track as possible during their time as students.

What if your church, like Notre Dame, could graduate fully

developed followers of Christ and then deploy them into a vast variety of different worlds? Imagine if those alumni could be connected into a cohesive, loyal network. Some might be businessmen, stay-at-home moms, teachers, lawyers, doctors, students, or social workers, all incarnating and impacting right where God has placed them. Imagine if your weekend worship gatherings were like home football games, where both students and alumni join together to celebrate what God is doing both inside the walls and out. Imagine that rather than having to strain to maintain financial resources from your existing student body, an ever-growing network of alumni generously and happily gave to perpetuate the environment that trained them to do what they are doing successfully in their own worlds beyond. That's quite an image, isn't it? Those are the new expectations we're embracing. More and more, we are trusting God to make us a kingdom boot camp and a university.

NEW TARGETS

We recognize that it's a little vague to say to people: "You should manifest your missional-incarnational impulse wherever you are." So we've begun to put some handles on that phrase. We've pinpointed seven areas we refer to as the domains of society, including the following:

- Health care
- Art
- Family
- Government
- Business
- Religion
- Education
- Justice

We are rearranging our access events around these domains of society as a way for people to take first steps in mission. By elevating these new targets we hope our people will understand that they don't really need us to mobilize them on mission with events because God has already mobilized them where they spend most of their time.

To unpack this further, let's look at the three common understandings of ministry in the church:

1. *Ministry = Clergy.* Ministry is done by trained professionals.
2. *Ministry = Volunteerism.* Ministry is something we do in our discretionary time.
3. *Ministry = Ordination of All Vocations.* All of life is our ministry.

The third understanding of ministry reflects a fresh emphasis on the idea that different domains or spheres of influence are avenues for God's work. This emphasis elevates and celebrates the ordination or calling of people to all different vocations in life. Ministry is more than just the work of paid professionals, and it is not simply something "extra" or optional to add onto our free time, separate and distinct from our careers and families. Instead, ministry is seen as something that we engage in every area of life. Since people do most of their living in one of the domains listed earlier, this means that most of their mission and ministry must and will happen as they live and work in that domain. This is the essence of incarnational ministry.

By explicitly identifying these domains and intentionally targeting them as avenues for ministry, we hope to foster teamwork and networking among our people. Access events often help to reveal who has what interest in each domain, and that can lead to additional momentum and relationships with other people who share the same interest.

NEW TOOLS

Any incarnational initiative will require tools that can get the job done. But if every missional expression needs staff and resources from "headquarters," we'll only be able to resource a very small number of ministries. We'll never see the church become a movement with that approach. That's why we focus on using our corporate resources to provide universally dividable resources like training, coaching, and technology so that everyone can have equal access and equal opportunity to succeed. So what are some of the tools we're rolling out?

- *A Training Track.* This is a process to help people discover and activate their missional-incarnational impulse. The goal is to help people discover the movement of God inside of them that is waiting to be unleashed. It's similar to a church diagnostic class (SHAPE, spiritual gifts assessments, etc.), but with a focus on incarnational living instead of volunteer roles.
- *Identify Coaches.* We are identifying successful practitioners in each domain of society who might serve as coaches for others.
- *Centralized Modeling.* By 2016, Granger will identify one grassroots initiative from each domain that we will support as an organized church. The goal is to showcase for others what is possible when an ordinary person says yes to their missional impulse.
- *Online Portal.* We are utilizing an online portal called The Table to get the organization of the church out of the way and allow people to connect and network directly for the purpose of community and shared mission.

NEW STORIES

As people take steps to live out their missional impulse, we're also lifting up the hero stories. Never underestimate the power of a good story! During one series, called "Picture This," we asked people to send us photos that summarize the mission God has called them to. We created a website for them to upload those photos, and then we printed them out and placed them at the front of our auditorium. This gave people an opportunity to see what others were doing and sparked many conversations. During another series, "Cow-Tipping," each week we shared stories of people who are seeking to live out "church as movement." To give you a taste of some of these stories, we've highlighted a few examples for you. These folks are our heroes!

Dan Adams: Jesus Knows Auto-CAD

Dan Adams and his brothers and sisters own and operate a family business that manufactures machines for a variety of automated tasks. They also provide a version of friction welding that is in high demand in certain industries throughout the world. Dan is a gifted leader and engineer, and together with his wife, who is also an engineer, they began looking for ways to own and incorporate the missional-incarnational impulse in their lives. At a morning meeting, Dan heard from a local business owner who had utilized his company as a means of impacting the community. He pitched an idea to his brothers and sisters at their firm, suggesting that they begin hiring people from the Monroe Circle community, offering vocational opportunities that would enable people to escape poverty and enter the workforce. Over a period of two years, Dan's company has offered a real-world laboratory for people with significant barriers to employment due to felony convictions or a lack of education, putting them on a track out of poverty and into independent living.

Joe Wisler: Jesus Gots Mad Skeellz

Joe has been around Granger since 1991, and he says, "I learned at Granger to live out a walk with Jesus in my day-to-day life." Joe's successful career in the sound industry helped him develop a unique skill set. Back in 2000, Joe began to ask himself, "How can I take these skills I've developed in the marketplace and infuse them with the mission of Jesus to benefit my community?" In 2008, at the peak of unemployment rates in Elkhart County, he met a man who had been asking the same question. This partnership led to the fulfillment of a dream, an organization called The Life Center of Elkhart County. The goal of this organization is to change lives through education.

Joe tells us, "Our goal is to teach biblical principles for all of life to at-risk youth and adults. We do that through vocational training, such as welding, auto mechanics, computer technology, business office communication, and customer service. It's basically a Bible-based leadership skill development track that has been operating for two years now. At first, we had no place to call home, but through what could only be described as a miracle, we were able to purchase five acres of land, and while the previous owner didn't want to sell at first, he ended up donating another four buildings on an additional thirty acres of land. God is good! We're seeing men who were on a path of returning to prison break substance addictions, get their GED, graduate from vocational training, and secure new jobs. We're just getting started, but we've already seen 30 percent of our students who graduate find meaningful employment. More than that, we've seen Jesus bringing new life to so many who were ready to give up."

Dan Blacketor: Jesus Loves Daughters

When the tsunami hit India back in 2004, Dan Blacketor became a volunteer leader for one of the Granger construction teams that traveled to the tsunami zone to help with rebuilding. On a subsequent trip in 2008, Dan had an experience that forever changed his life. "We stopped at a small town called Dharmapuri. As I got out of the car, an Indian family was coming up from the river just having drowned their newborn baby daughter. I was aware of infanticide, a practice fueled by the caste system and the associated traditions, where baby girls are seen as a liability and murdered at birth. But until that moment, I couldn't believe this horrific practice still occurred."

Over the next three months, Dan learned that the problem was bigger than he had first realized. Over ten million girls die each year from infanticide in South Asia. Dan wasn't sure there was anything he could do. But the memory of that experience in India just wouldn't let him go, so he returned to India three months later to meet with people who were working on solutions to the problem, and to visit several villages where the practice was common.

Dan continues: "In one village, where every single family had killed a daughter, I met a young mother with a newborn. Finding out that it was a girl baby, we learned her life would hang in the balance until she received a name. Being the only white boy from the US in town, I was something of a visiting celebrity. So my Indian friend, Raj, created an opportunity to save the girl. He said to me, 'Give her a name and celebrate her birth with a small financial gift.' We threw out three names to the family, and the kids chose Rhema. I held her, said a quick prayer for her, and tucked a couple of bucks in her diaper. Then I handed several more bills to her young mother. That little act shocked the whole village, demonstrating a baby girl's life had value and worth. That small gift gave Rhema a chance at life. That's it.

"Coming home from that trip, I knew that God had given me an answer to my prayers. I saw that God had equipped me with just enough knowledge and life experiences to change the fate of that one little girl. That very night we launched The Rhema Project, a movement of friends committed to rescuing more babies like Rhema. We started with Rhema's village, where two years ago, more than thirty-five girls were killed shortly after birth simply because they were female. Today, after a few small initiatives and with the help of friends, no baby girls have been murdered in the last three months!"

Ted Bryant: Jesus Loves Leftovers

Six years ago, Ted was working on his PhD at Notre Dame, and he decided to go on a mission trip with the youth group at Granger to visit some orphanages in Mexico. The team needed to fill forty suitcases full of school supplies to give away to the orphans, and

Ted remembers thinking, "Wow! That's a lot of pencils—how are we going to do that?" In the coming days, Ted said to God, "Lord, give me an idea that will cause a problem ... that we'll have so many supplies we won't be able to fit them all in the suitcases!" Ted now realizes that he had no idea what he was asking for! Later that week, Ted was thinking about his own school days, and he remembered the locker clean-out days at the end of every year. This memory sparked an idea: "What if, instead of students throwing away everything, I provided different containers—next to the trash cans—so that they could put new or slightly used school supplies, books, and clothes into them for recycled redistribution to people who can't afford them?" It was a simple but brilliant idea, and best of all it empowered student leadership in local schools. Student leaders carried out the project, reversing an out-of-control culture of waste and saving thousands of pounds of garbage from heading to the landfill. At the same time, the resources saved provide hope for the neediest in our communities and an opportunity for every student to give back to their own community without ever having to leave school— or buy anything! This idea prompted Ted to launch an organization called GreenLockers to handle the supplies and redistribution. To date, GreenLockers has doubled in size and scope, going from two schools the first year to thirty-four schools and more than sixteen thousand pounds of sorted supplies collected in 2009. These supplies are given away to charities all across Michiana and to several international partners in Mexico and India.

Kristin Baker: Jesus at a Chalkboard

Before switching careers, Kristin was a high school teacher in the public schools for ten years. She loved every minute of her job— except for lunchtime in the teachers' lounge! Her time in the classroom was wonderful, but she would notice during lunch break that her peers looked like worn-out survivors of battle, not energized leaders. Burnout was leading to bitterness, and she grew sad and frustrated hearing teachers refer to students as worthless idiots. She began to realize that most of the teachers weren't villains; they were victims of a flawed system. "There were several programs for at-risk kids," Kristin recalls, "but who encourages the at-risk teachers? Who is there to remind them *they* matter and their purpose is worth the work?" In Kristin's experience, the teachers were often treated like children, or as they often referred to themselves, "guards in a prison." Kristin started dreaming and began asking, "What if high school was actually something to look forward to, for both teachers and students? Something that was engaging and felt more like a family than an institution? What if teachers were helped and encouraged on a regular basis more than they were reprimanded?" Kristin's dreams led her to begin volunteering every Friday helping teachers with anything and everything they couldn't get around to, organizing and grading, leading creative writing workshops, and working with their toughest troublemakers one-on-one. Though she used to dread lunchtime because of all the negativity, it has now become her favorite part of the day! "I bring in treats for the teachers, listen and encourage these incredible people who have the weight of future generations on their shoulders and a tough crowd to face every fifty-five minutes. They say 'hurt people hurt people,' but I believe better-loved people, love people better. I may not be able to single-handedly turn around the public education monster, but it's a little yeast in the dough ... and every little pocket has lift."

So where is Granger Community Church in these stories? On Sunday, you'll find all of us gathering together in our buildings. But come Monday, Granger Community Church is spread throughout the community: working in doctors' offices and hospitals, laying pipe and swinging hammers on construction sites, educating in preschools and university classrooms, working in corporate offices, and flipping on the open signs at scores of small businesses all over our community.

And the same is true of your church. Every week, believers take the church with them into the world because they *are* the church. We don't "go to church"; Jesus designed us to be "church on the go." Jesus intends the church to be an advancing, undomesticated, revolutionary force that is pushing back the forces of hell. When Jesus says, "I will build my church, and the gates of Hades will not overcome it" (Matt. 16:18), we know that he is absolutely confident about what he can build and do through your people. The question for you, as church leaders, is, "Do you believe it?" If you catch the vision of Jesus, your focus will shift away from your programs, and you will declare to your people with your time, energy, and resources: "You can do it; we can help."

Chapter 15

FROM GREAT COMMISSION TO GREAT COMPLETION

Missional Move 15

If you're a parent, you hate that question every child asks when the trip in the car lasts longer than ten minutes: "Are we there yet?" Since you've made it this far, you know that we've covered a lot of ground. We've looked at how we are attempting to join God on his mission. We've looked at the missional moves necessary to change a church so it is able and ready to engage in that mission. And we've unpacked the strategy and tactics, theology and praxis that we've brought to bear in our own journey.

Like everyone who follows Christ, we believe that one day all of this will end. One day the kingdom will fully come, and we will look at one another with a sweaty smile, clap each other on the shoulder, and run together into the presence of our King! The Great Commission does, in fact, have an end point. It began two thousand years ago (though as we've seen, it truly started in Genesis 12), and at some point, the Great Commission will become the Great Completion, and God will receive maximum glory throughout the whole world (G3!).

Like our own children, we are tempted to ask our Father, "Are we there yet?" The answer right now is still no. With 1.2 billion people yet to hear the gospel, it might seem as if we will never get there. But consider that for every unreached people group in the world, there are five hundred Bible-believing local churches.[1] A movement of local churches and the people of God on mission do indeed have the resources to finish the Great Commission.

We began our journey together by looking at the move from Saved Souls to Saved Wholes, a move that celebrates the lordship of Jesus Christ. Now we end with a missional move that anticipates the final outcome of his lordship—the completion of the Great Commission. But how do we move from Great Commission to Great Completion? Or to put it another way, How do we, as local churches, become strategic in our thinking, moving the kingdom ball farther down the field toward the end zone of G3? We believe that the answer lies in four strategic pursuits: capacity building, focusing on unreached people groups, empowering apostolically gifted people groups, and finally, through what we call compound interest.

CAPACITY BUILDING

We believe that the training of reproducing networks of indigenous church planters will be one of the keys to fulfilling the Great Commission. Indigenous leaders serve more effectively than foreign workers. They are more rapidly deployed and more easily sustained than the traditional vision with its waves of long-term, cross-cultural missionaries. We believe there are still places in the world where the expertise of trained cross-cultural missionaries is absolutely critical. But in many places, the time has come for those of us in the West to move from front-line focus to supply line. Many will still be called to go and serve cross-culturally, but rather than going to the front line, with direct ministry as the priority, we will serve as supply training for indigenous leadership, helping people to lead in their own communities.

Again, this shifting emphasis should not discount the painstaking sacrifice and work of the men and women who have dared to cross seas and cultures to bring the gospel to places that would not have heard it otherwise. The past global season did not allow most churches to be personally engaged in the work. Western missionary movements were mobilized to reach the rest of the world, and the effectiveness of that past missionary movement led to an indigenous church in every geographic nation. This is a historic moment in the history of the church.

This new reality is ushering in a massive shift. In this twenty-first century world, everything has changed. Now, for the first time in history, the local church throughout the world is ready and strategically positioned to reach the unreached in every nation and people group. The focus of our engagement, as churches in the global North and West, will need to continually be reevaluated and changed. A well-known guide to global prayer, *Operation World*, summarizes it this way: "The concept of Christianity as a European 'white man's religion' is demonstrably a myth. Though sometimes small in number, all but concealed, or mostly members of a minority people group, there are now Christians living in fellowship in every country on earth. World mission, globalization and high migration rates have dispersed the church into every corner of the world, both to previously unevangelized areas and back to traditionally Christian regions where the church is in sharp decline."[2]

To personalize what we are saying, we'd like to introduce you to a friend named Mohan. Mohan is an electrical engineer who works a normal workweek like you and I would. But unlike us, he spends his weekend planting a church among the Malayali, an unreached people. Near the area where he lives in southern India, the Malayali people live on a remote mountaintop. On Friday evening, Mohan takes a bus from his hometown as far as it will take him. After that, he hikes ten kilometers, seven of them straight up a mountain. We've made this trek with Mohan, and it's no tiptoe through the tulips!

Mohan explained to us, "The first three months, I made the trip every weekend, but no one in the village would even speak to me or even acknowledge my presence." Can you imagine making a trip like this every weekend with no results? When I first heard this, I thought of myself and realize I would have likely given up by week two.

After three months, Mohan began to bring little presents to the village, leaving rice and other small items for the people. The gifts led to a breakthrough when a family reached out to him and took him in for a meal. One of the first questions the family asked him was, "How do you make it up the mountain alive at night? Does not the demon god attack you?" Mohan learned that the people of the village live in perpetual fear of a local deity who forbids them to travel at night outside the village. They told Mohan, "At night the evil spirits fill the mountainside. You can hear them rumbling in the rocks at night." With boldness and hope, Mohan shared the good news of Jesus with them: "This is why I have come. The one true God has sent me to tell you of his Son who can bring you freedom." Mohan went on to explain the gospel to the family, but sadly, they showed little interest in what he had to say.

When Mohan returned the next weekend, however, the family was eagerly waiting for him. They grabbed him by the hand and said, "Tell us more about your God. We know he must be the true God!" Surprised at their questions, Mohan asked them how they knew this, and they replied with joy: "Since you left last weekend, we have not heard the demon gods. For years, we have heard the rocks rumble outside the village each night. But these last seven nights, it is silent. All we know is that the news of your Jesus has frightened the other gods away." Perhaps all of this was just a strange geological coincidence—or perhaps God was at work, confirming the message of the gospel in ways that made sense to the Malayali people!

Today a church of more than forty Malayali gather on that mountainside to worship each week. Mohan shared his vision for the church with us. "One of those early nights before anyone would receive me, I collapsed in exhaustion halfway up the mountain, saying, 'I am ready to give up, Lord.'" Mohan continued, "Jesus appeared to me that night. I saw him with my own eyes standing before me. He said, 'Mohan, if I loved these people enough to die for them, the least you can do is climb up this mountain.'" In that moment, Mohan said, "My heart exploded with joy! I knew this village would know Christ and they in turn would go from this village to reach the other tribes in this region." That vision is now a reality.

Wherever you go in the world today, there is a "Mohan" waiting for you. Knowing that changes everything. As leaders in the West, we must be willing to take whatever influence we have and leverage that to elevate the status of these indigenous leaders. Though we may not be involved in direct, frontline work, we are being called by God to spend time providing specific expertise, training, and infrastructure and administrative support. We dedicate ourselves to training "Mohans" so that they can distribute that training to the networks themselves. Most of the church planters we train at the most basic level will successfully plant a church of between twenty and fifty people within a year to eighteen months, and these churches typically plant another one to three daughter churches. That kind of replication is simply not possible without our external missionary involvement, and it has convinced us that God wants to use us in this new role of equipping, supporting, and supplying indigenous leaders.

FOCUS ON UNREACHED PEOPLE

Unreached people groups (UPGs) are another natural point of focus for local churches committed to the G3 ballgame. In the third missional move ("From My Tribe to Every Tribe"), we talked about the importance of "people group thinking." Typically, an unreached people group is defined as a people group where fewer than 2 percent of the population are evangelical Christ-followers. Because we understand that the kingdom will not be fully present until all people groups have had an opportunity to be represented at the table of the King, we want to spend the bulk of our G3 efforts focusing there.

We are not saying to every church or every church leader reading this book that you should focus on UPGs. However, we believe the current hour calls for local churches that are willing go to the hard places to reach people in strategic positions of influence, and one of the best ways to do this is through a focus on an unreached people group. So how do you go about reaching an unreached people group? You can't just wander into the jungle and start asking the people you meet if they're unreached, right? More than ever, the critical nature of transformational partnership becomes clear. A local church here will often need a broker who can build a bridge for the church with indigenous Christian leaders. Often, this will happen through partner organizations or missionaries who already have relationships with the networks on the ground.

We have found that the best way to connect with an unreached people group is an indirect approach: through adjacent people groups (APGs) or proximal people groups (PPGs). An adjacent people group is a reached people group that is geographically and/ or culturally positioned to a place of "nearness" to an unreached one. A proximal people group is one step further out from an adjacent people group. Though the proximal group may still possess enough of the core culture, language, and heritage to be effective in the absence of an adjacent people group, it will probably have to work a little harder at getting there.

Mohan's story, which we shared earlier, is a good illustration of what we mean. Mohan is culturally and geographically proximal to the Malayali. Mohan and the Malayali are both from Dravidian class people groups, so they share a common cultural and linguistic lexicon. The Malayali people are still technically considered an unreached group. However, now that the Malayali on Mohan's mountain are becoming more and more "reached," they are traveling to share the gospel with other communities on the nearby mountains who are also unreached. The village that Mohan reached has become a strategic adjacent people group, currently pastored by a man from a proximal people group (Mohan). It's a PPG working with a UPG to become an APG to reach another UPG. Wow, that's a lot of acronyms! Hopefully, you get the point.

EMPOWERING APOSTOLICALLY GIFTED PEOPLE GROUPS

At Granger, we focus our capacity building on what we have learned to call *apostolically gifted* people groups. Just as individuals are apostolically gifted by God to take the gospel where it has not yet gone, we also believe that entire people groups can also be apostolically gifted by God. That's not to say that everyone in the people group has the exact same gifts, of course. But it is to say that the tendency toward this apostolic strength appears in certain people groups at an unusually high rate.

In southern India, for instance, we are certain that there are very shy, introverted people who would rather stay home and keep to themselves. However, they are in the minority in comparison to the vast numbers of gregarious, colorful, expressive people who tend to pervade the Dravidian people groups of that region. As a result, when Dravidians own the gospel message at a deep level, they tend to scattergun it … well … everywhere they go. They can't help it. They are expressive and mobile, and they adapt well to other environments and cultures. They seem to be supernaturally gifted by God to go, send, and spread. They are what we would call an apostolically gifted people group.

The Dravidians work mainly in Southeast Asia and North America, the Middle East and Africa. They maintain ties with one another and yet also develop friendships quickly with people wherever they find themselves. As a result of this, and despite the fact that India itself is one of the most unreached geopolitical nations on the planet, the Dravidians have become a missionary force having an amazing effect in the world. Again, *Operation World* summarizes what we are saying about the Indian church: "Today, over 1,000

Indian mission agencies and church-based initiatives have sent out over 100,000 church planters, evangelists and social workers—many of them cross-culturally—and have planted tens of thousands of Christ-following congregations. Considerable thought and practice are now shaping the Indian Church and society that can follow Christ and live out the Gospel in a contextualized fashion."[3]

And they are not alone! Like our brothers and sisters in India, we believe God has scattered these apostolically gifted people groups strategically around the world. Ron VanderGriend and Dave Stravers (the current CEO of Mission India) first defined this concept for us. Apostolically gifted people groups, they say, have the following characteristics:

"They have an awareness of the mission history that brought them to Christ." They know that they are the beneficiaries of "sent ones" who came to them, and so they own and understand their responsibility to do likewise. In India, our friend Raj can tell you the story of the missionary who first came to his people group. The man's name was Ziegenwald, and he came to India from Germany to give his life for Raj's people. Raj says, "When I am feeling discouraged, I go to the cemetery where Ziegenwald is buried. There, I sit next to his grave and think about all that he had to endure to bring my people the gospel of Jesus. This man left his country, his home, and everything that he knew as familiar to come and die with and for my people. Then I pray and ask God to help me to be like Ziegenwald, and my spirits are refreshed. I leave from that place ready to enter the battle again." Ziegenwald did not win Raj, but his work still directly impacts him on a daily basis. Raj feels the weight of that missionary mantle placed upon his shoulders, and he carries it forward with diligence and responsibility in his everyday life.

"They have an understanding of the story of how they received the biblical text." When I asked Raj about the history of Bible translation for his people group in Tamilnadu, Raj's brilliant dark eyes ignited with passion as he told the story of Ziegenwald's learning

the rudiments of the Tamil language on his passage from Germany to South India so that he could translate the Bible for his people. Before dying at a young age, Ziegenwald successfully translated the New Testament and the Old Testament through the book of Ruth.

HEAR FOR YOURSELF

Visit *missionalmoves.com* and listen to Raj tell the story of how Ziegenwald came to South India and impacted his people group, resulting in a wave of missional passion that has extended even to this day. Look for "The Story behind an Apostolically Gifted People Group."

"They experience or have a history of persecution." One night, while bumping around in the back of a Tata Sumo four-wheel drive with Raj, we asked, "Raj, how many of our church planters in India will have experienced some form of overt persecution for their faith?" He was silent for a moment and then answered, "Probably about 50 percent of our pastors even right now are experiencing some form of overt persecution. Out of those 50 percent, many will experience the loss of a job, be ridiculed by their families and friends, and potentially even be chased out of their homes or towns. In the more extreme cases, families will actually hold funerals for them and tell them that they are no longer alive to them. However, about half of that 50 percent will experience persecution that is much more severe. They will be beaten, raped, or will have to be continually on their guard against other acts of violence. It is understood here that if you are a pastor or a Christ-follower, persecution is just an accepted part of the process."

"They have some social factor that makes them travel and/or communicate beyond their borders." There is something about apostolically gifted people groups that makes them freely mobile and unafraid to bridge cultural gaps. We cannot tell you the number of friends we have in southern India who have spouses, children, or other relatives who work in Dubai, Qatar, Saudi Arabia, South America, Kuwait, Yemen, Libya, the Philippines, China, or even in the northern part of India itself or beyond to Tibet, Bhutan, and

Nepal. In our community here in South Bend, Indiana, there are doctors from Chennai, business owners from Kerala and Karnataka (other southern Indian states in India), and children in our kids' classes whose parents are from various places throughout southern India as well. And it's no coincidence. Many ethnologists believe that the Dravidian people groups of southern India are the origin point for most of the "Gypsy" cultures throughout Eastern Europe (including the famous Romany of Romania, Bulgaria, and Hungary). They are a mobile people on the go.

We're not claiming apostolically gifted people groups are some-how more valuable than any other people group. Their gifting just makes them strategic for working with unreached people groups. Here are several examples of other apostolically gifted people groups based on Ron and Dave's work overseeing the planting of more than twenty-five thousand churches in fifty nations.

Burmese Karen (pronounced Kah-rin). When the British colo-nized what is modern-day Myanmar (old-world Burma), they selected a particular people group called the Karen to aid them in much of their indigenous administrative work. The reason for this is that the Karen traveled easily from place to place, adapted to local customs and nuances from village to village, and were able to also integrate with the British themselves to understand empire goals and objectives. Today many Karen have come to Christ (some figures are as high as 40 percent) but are heavily persecuted and have had to flee overt violence against them. They migrated across the Thai or surrounding borders, and many have made transitions to the United States and other Western nations as well.

Filipino. With a population of 93.6 million people, the Philip-pines is the eighth-largest missionary-sending nation in the world (just behind the UK and Canada).[4] But beyond that statistic, what is even more compelling is the notion that much of the actual mis-sionary activity never occurs "on the books" in any overt capacity. In one ministry training program, participants train as household butlers, cooks, and nannies for the purpose of traveling throughout the world. Many gain positions of influence within the homes of those with wealth but who have not yet entered the kingdom of God. In addition, based on our own travels, we have seen Filipino nationals working not only throughout Southeast Asia but also as far away as Western Europe and even Central and South America.

Nigerian Igbo (pronounced Ee-boh). While helping with the initial concept for a Manga (think "Japanese comic book") version of the Bible in 2005, we (Rob, Jack, and Ron) were walking the streets of Tokyo one night for a bit of sightseeing. A dark-skinned man approached us to see if we wanted to purchase any of the prostitutes that he was selling. Without missing a beat, Ron listened to the man's accent and then said, "You're from Nigeria, aren't you?" The man's eyes widened and he looked at the towering mountain of a man who had addressed him (Ron is six foot seven and weighs 270 pounds). "You're Igbo, aren't you?" "Yes," the man replied as he put the literature he was selling away. Ron smiled at the man and said, "Does your grandmother know what you're doing here?" The man lowered his gaze shamefully and started to stammer. Ron continued, "You were taught better than this, my brother. Your grandmother took you to church as a boy. You learned the stories of Scripture. Your people—the Igbo people—are followers of the One True God. Why are you here in this foreign land peddling prostitutes?" The man admitted as much, quickly ended the conversation, and made a hasty retreat. Ron turned to us and explained, "The Igbo people are apostolically gifted. They go everywhere. Nigeria is one of the largest missionary-sending African nations." We nodded. "How many Africans have you seen here in Tokyo?" Ron asked. We remarked that in the couple of days we hadn't seen any who looked dark-skinned or spoke with African accents. "And yet the Igbo are here," Ron continued, "even in the midst of a land where you would think you would not find them."

As we pursue resourcing networks of indigenous church planters to reach the maximum number of unreached people groups, we are attempting to align ourselves whenever possible with apostolically gifted people groups. We believe that they have been supernaturally engineered by God to blaze new trails for the kingdom where its message has not yet gone. May the apostolic genius resident within them be fully realized as local churches in the West seek to amplify and support their impact!

COMPOUND INTEREST

As the prophet says, don't despise the day of small beginnings! Western churches are tempted to go big. Big conference! Big campaigns! Big projects! But in the kingdom, big is small and small is big. In other words, we would encourage you to start small and stay small, keeping the focus on reproducing. Focus on a small group of indigenous leaders. Help them to succeed by building capacity and then, most importantly, help them reproduce themselves.

Don't fall for the temptation to go "fast" either. In the kingdom, fast is slow and slow is fast. What starts out small and slow, if faithfully reproduced and methodically executed, may turn the world into the kind of place that Jesus talked about with his disciples. The kingdom starts small and slowly, but it grows into something massive.

At the 2011 Exponential Conference in Orlando, Florida, author and organic church guru Neil Cole spoke about the concept that movements start small and slow. He explained it using the concept of compound interest. You start with a small investment that slowly grows over the years, building off the initial investment and the subsequent earnings, compounded together over time. Often, by the time you see something that looks like a substantial movement, it has been compounding and growing steadily and faithfully beneath the visible surface for years. Small, faithfully reproducing nodes have collected into networks that have now become a larger movement. If we simply and faithfully continue to pursue the work that God calls us to do, the principle of compound interest will lead us to see

the Great Commission become the Great Completion someday—
possibly within the lifetime of our own children! Sound crazy?
Maybe. But even if we are wrong, the kingdom is still growing and
the clock will continue ticking ahead on the timetable of redemptive
history. God will continue his work—but will we be involved in what
he is doing? Today we know that God is doing something new, and
today is our opportunity to respond and get involved.

WHERE WE GO FROM HERE

We believe that the missional moves we have highlighted are evidence that something profound is operating beneath the ocean of
our reality in the Western church. We see the seismic nature of
these shifts and how they are beginning to affect the global body
of Christ. We see potential energy building within God's people,
energy that is waiting to surge forth and create a new tsunami of
God's love and peace and salvation. For our part, we welcome the
opportunity to be part of the rising tide—whether it's rising in our
own back yard or at the bleeding edge of the Great Commission.

As we close, we want to leave you with one last concept, something that we speak about often in our life together. Hopefully,
you have become somewhat accustomed to the rather quirky mix
of metaphors and pictures that we use to help us make sense of all
this. Here is one more. Miyamoto Musashi was perhaps the greatest swordsman Japan has ever seen. In Thomas Cleary's translation
of Musashi's literary classic, *The Book of Five Rings*,[5] we read about
a Japanese concept called *shin-ken*. Literally, the words mean "real
sword." The phrase is derived from the feudal era of that nation
when swordsmanship was still a very necessary field of study for a
samurai warrior. When sparring with a friend or instructor, a samurai could afford to be a bit sloppy since students would only practice
with *bokken*, wooden swords. A *bokken*, though made of wood, is
created from fired hardwood, so it still leaves a mark. If you miss

a block and are smacked in the head, the injury would most likely result in a bruise or bump, but not serious injury or death.

The moment that a samurai warrior steps onto a field of battle, however, things change. It is now time for *shin-ken*, the real sword. If you step incorrectly, miss a block, or fail to discern the correct timing for a strike, you will lose your life. Today this concept still survives in Japan even though the days of samurai warriors and real swords have passed, and *shin-ken* now means, "doing something with deadly earnest." It implies that you bring all that you have in you to accomplish a goal, even if it costs you your life to do so.

We recognize Paul sounding out his *shin-ken* cry in Acts 20:24, when he writes, "I consider my life worth nothing to me; my only aim is to finish the race and complete the task the Lord Jesus has given me—the task of testifying to the good news of God's grace."

So what's your *shin-ken* cry?

As the people of God, our hearts burn with a desire to see the reign and rule of the true King, Jesus, advance in the world today. And as followers and subjects of the King, we have a part in bringing that reality to bear, seeing God's will be done on earth as it is in heaven. Our earnest desire is to wake up each morning and put away the wooden practice swords, approaching the day with our real sword in hand, ready to give our lives, if necessary, for the sake of the gospel and the global glory of God. This is a kingdom mindset—a *shin-ken* mindset—and it's our answer to the call to take up our cross and follow Jesus, our Lord and Savior. We are grateful that you have chosen to join us on this path. You have our respect and admiration. And we look forward to the day when we will be together with you, joining people from every tribe and nation, as the reverse tsunami of God's global glory covers every square inch of the cosmos. May that day come soon!

In the meantime, however, we look forward to seeing you on the field!

NOTES

INTRODUCTION

1. "The Deadliest Tsunami in History?" National Geographic News, January 7, 2005, *http://news.nationalgeographic.com/news/2004/12/1227_041226_tsunami.html*.
2. Mark Twain, *A Connecticut Yankee in King Arthur's Court*.

CHAPTER 1: FROM SAVED SOULS TO SAVED WHOLES

1. A phrase birthed from the genius of Alan Hirsch.
2. Our take on what has been proposed in many formats. Scot McKnight offers a six-part version of the biblical narrative in *The Blue Parakeet: Rethinking How You Read the Bible*. N. T. Wright offers a five-act play in his article "How Is the Bible Authoritative?" and his book *The Last Word: Beyond the Bible Wars to a New Understanding of the Authority of Scripture*. John Eldridge describes it in four parts in his book *Epic: The Story of God and Your Role in It*.
3. John H. Walton, *The Lost World of Genesis One: Ancient Cosmology and the Origins Debate* (Downers Grove, Ill.: InterVarsity, 2009).

4. John Ortberg, "If Jesus Ran the World," sermon, September 18, 2002.

5. Cornelius Plantinga Jr., *Not the Way It's Supposed to Be: A Breviary of Sin* (Grand Rapids, Mich.: Eerdmans, 1995), 10.

CHAPTER 2: FROM MISSIONS TO MISSION

1. Alan Hirsch and Debra Hirsch, *Untamed: Reactivating a Missional Form of Discipleship* (Grand Rapids, Mich.: Baker, 2010), Kindle edition, location 1384.

2. Ed Silvoso, *That None Should Perish: How to Reach Entire Cities for Christ through Prayer Evangelism* (Ventura, Calif.: Regal, 1995).

3. J. J. Durham, *Exodus*, WBC 3 (Dallas: Word, 1987), 260.

4. Roland Allen, *The Spontaneous Expansion of the Church* (London: World Dominion Press, 1927), 131. Many of the quotes and thoughts in this section have been strongly influenced by "The Missional Church," a dissertation paper by one of our mentors, Don Golden.

CHAPTER 3: FROM MY TRIBE TO EVERY TRIBE

1. John Piper, "The Radical Cost of Following Jesus," sermon, October 27, 2002.

2. We have long called Matthew 28:18–19 the Great Commission. But as we mentioned earlier, it's actually "the Great Re-commission." This is a brilliant term coined by Bob Sjogren in his book *Unveiled At Last: Discover God's Hidden Message from Genesis to Revelation* (Seattle: YWAM Publishing, 1992), 50. We highly recommend Bob's book, which was hugely instructive to us when it came to the concepts of the Great Re-commission, "people group thinking," and God's global glory. Reading this book changed the way we read the Bible.

3. Don Richardson, *Eternity in Their Hearts: Startling Evidence of Belief in the One True God in Hundreds of Cultures throughout the World*, 3d ed. (Ventura, Calif.: Regal, 2005), 137–48.

4. Bob Sjogren, *The Story of the Bible*, *www.unveilinglory.com/youteach/pdf/Notes-The_Story_of_the_Bible_1.pdf*.

5. We often miss the G3 storyline and the two tracks of God's promise to Abraham because it falls outside our visual range. We are conditioned to reading the Bible in bits and pieces, but this unites our understanding around the larger storyline of the Scriptures. If you're ready to dig deeper, we have a G3 map, which provides the ten-thousand-foot view of the story.

6. Lera Boroditsky, "How Does Our Language Shape the Way We Think?"

June 12, 2009, *http://www.edge.org/3rd_culture/boroditsky09/boroditsky09_index.html*.

7. Ibid.

8. "Maps in Our Minds — RadioLab WNYC's Radio Lab," *Lost & Found*, Season 9, Episode 2, January 25, 2011.

9. Ibid.

10. On a few occasions it is used to refer to a whole tribe (Jer. 8:3; Amos 3:1–2).

11. Gen. 18:18; 22:18; 26:4; 28:14–15.

12. There are four predominant ways to look at people groups. (1) *Blocs of People.* The blocs of people approach looks for big blocs that provide a limited number of summary categories, like major cultural and affinity blocs. (2) *Ethnolinguistic Peoples.* This approach divides into ethnic groups that self-identify through traditions of descent, history, customs, and language. See the Joshua Project for a listing of these groups: www.joshuaproject.com. (3) *Sociopeoples.* This is a small association of people who have an affinity based upon shared interest, activity, or occupation. This refers to the distinction we made earlier between *mispachot* and *ethne*, which we will address in a later missional move. (4) *Unimax People Groups.* Ralph Winter defines it this way: "A unimax people is the maximum-sized group sufficiently unified to be the target of a single people movement to Christ, where 'unified' refers to the fact that there are no significant barriers of either understanding or acceptance to stop the spread of the gospel. For evangelistic purposes [a people group] is 'the largest group within which the gospel can spread as a church planting movement without encountering barriers of understanding or acceptance'" ("Finishing the Task," *www.joshuaproject.net/assets/FinishingTheTask.pdf*).

CHAPTER 4: FROM OR TO AND

1. Of course, we could inundate you with statistics, but that's not the purpose of this book. Needless to say, the times they are changing. Only 15 percent of American churches are growing, and fewer than 5 percent are growing by conversion. In a recent ten-year period, ten thousand American churches disappeared.

CHAPTER 5: FROM THE CENTER TO THE MARGINS

1. Rom. 3:23.

2. Neil Cole, *Organic Church* (San Francisco: Jossey-Bass, 2005).

CHAPTER 6: FROM TOP DOWN TO BOTTOM UP

1. Henry Blackaby, etal., *Experiencing God: Knowing and Doing the Will of God* (workbook) (Nashville: Lifeway, 2007), 101.

CHAPTER 9: FROM RELIEF TO DEVELOPMENT

1. Steve Corbett and Brian Fikkert, *When Helping Hurts* (Chicago: Moody, 2009), 105.

CHAPTER 10: FROM PROFESSIONALS TO FULL PARTICIPATION

1. Neil Cole, *Organic Church* (San Francisco: Jossey-Bass, 2005), 128–29.
2. Captain D. Michael Abrashoff, *It's Your Ship: Management Techniques from the Best Damn Ship in the Navy* (New York: Business Plus, 2002), 6.

CHAPTER 11: FROM FORMAL TO FRACTAL LEADERSHIP

1. Neil Cole, *Organic Church: Growing Faith Where Life Happens* (San Francisco: Jossey-Bass, 2005).
2. Wayne Cordeiro, *Doing Church as a Team* (Ventura, Calif.: Regal, 2009).

CHAPTER 12: FROM INSTITUTION TO MOVEMENT

1. Alan Hirsch, *The Forgotten Ways: Reactivating the Missional Church* (Grand Rapids, Mich.: Brazos, 2009).
2. We understand this is a massive claim. You'll need to dig in and decide for yourself. Alan doesn't claim to have discovered something new. Instead, he sees himself as the custodian of something given to him by grace through the study of Scripture and historical apostolic movements. He further suggests that while apostolic movements might have "more than the six elements, they never will have less than the six elements." Based on our experience in India and our own research, we wholeheartedly agree.
3. Alan Hirsch and Dave Ferguson, *On the Verge* (Grand Rapids, Mich.: Zondervan, 2011), 115.
4. Ibid., 42–43.

CHAPTER 13: FROM MEGA AND MULTI TO MEGA, MULTI, AND MICRO

1. Alan Hirsch and Dave Ferguson, *On the Verge* (Grand Rapids, Mich.: Zondervan, 2011), 64.

2. Thomas Kuhn, *The Structure of Scientific Revolutions* (Chicago: Phoenix, 1962).

3. Todd Wilson, "A Micro Manifesto," May 20, 2010, toddwilson.org. Todd's manifesto has strongly influenced the language and the framework for this chapter. Todd is one of the most influential church leaders in America whom you probably have never heard of. He is a man who operates "behind the curtain" with no concern for recognition or praise, currently creating what we believe may be the nexus for the next great move of God here in America. I'd tell you more about him, but we've been sworn to secrecy.

4. *http://www.markbeeson.com/mark_beeson/2008/03/it-is-easter-we.html.*

5. Gen. 1:28 (NLT).

6. Robert Coleman, *The Master Plan of Evangelism* (Grand Rapids, Mich.: Revell, 1934, 1963, 1993), 89.

7. *www.revealnow.com.* REVEAL is a five-year study, led by the Willow Creek Association, of 280,000 congregants in twelve hundred churches across a wide variety of denominations. The bottom-line learning was that church activity is not a blueprint for spiritual growth. So while we've been working so hard to create a "church-building and program-centric" approach to disciple making, this study truly revealed that those systems aren't producing the results we hoped for.

8. Tony Dale, Felicity Dale, and George Barna, *The Rabbit and the Elephant: Why Small Is the New Big for Today's Church* (Wheaton, Ill.: Tyndale, 2009).

9. Ibid., Kindle edition, location 176.

10. Ibid., emphasis added.

11. Verge Network blog series *Missional Communities: 7 Frequently Asked Questions,* *http://www.vergenetwork.org/2010/12/30/hugh-halter-what-is-a-missional-community-printable/.*

12. Verge Network blog series, *Missional Communities: 7 Frequently Asked Questions,* *http://www.vergenetwork.org/2011/01/07/jeff-vanderstelt-what-is-a-missional-community-printable/.*

13. Verge Network blog series, *Missional Communities: 7 Frequently Asked Questions,* *http://www.vergenetwork.org/2010/12/31/mike-breen-what-is-a-missional-community-printable/.*

CHAPTER 14: FROM "WE CAN DO IT; YOU CAN HELP" TO "YOU CAN DO IT; WE CAN HELP"

1. Alan Hirsch, *The Forgotten Ways: Reactivating the Missional Church* (Grand Rapids, Mich.: Brazos Press, 2009), 36–37.

2. Michael Frost and Alan Hirsch, *The Shaping of Things to Come* (Grand Rapids, Mich.: Baker, 2004), 35.

3. Hirsch, *Forgotten Ways*, 128.

CHAPTER 15: FROM GREAT COMMISSION TO GREAT COMPLETION

1. *http://www.missionfrontiers.org/issue/article/become-an-adopt-a-people-advocate.*

2. Jason Mandryk, *Operation World*, 7th ed. (Colorado Springs: Biblica, 2010), 5.

3. Ibid., 408–9.

4. Ibid., 951.

5. Miyamoto Musashi, *The Book of Five Rings*, trans. Thomas Cleary (Boston: Shambhala, 2000).